The New York Times

LOOKING FORWARD

Energy Technology

THE TOOLS OF THE INDUSTRY

EDUCATIONAL PUBLISHING
BOOKS

THE NEW YORK TIMES EDITORIAL STAFF

Published in 2020 by New York Times Educational Publishing
in association with The Rosen Publishing Group, Inc.
29 East 21st Street, New York, NY 10010

First Edition

The New York Times
Alex Ward: Editorial Director, Book Development
Phyllis Collazo: Photo Rights/Permissions Editor
Heidi Giovine: Administrative Manager

Rosen Publishing
Megan Kellerman: Managing Editor
Greg Clinton: Editor
Greg Tucker: Creative Director
Brian Garvey: Art Director

Cataloging-in-Publication Data
Names: New York Times Company.
Title: Energy technology: the tools of the industry / edited by the New York Times editorial staff.
Description: New York : New York Times Educational Publishing, 2020. | Series: Looking forward | Includes glossary and index.
Identifiers: ISBN 9781642822632 (library bound) | ISBN 9781642822625 (pbk.) | ISBN 9781642822649 (ebook)
Subjects: LCSH: Power resources—Juvenile literature. | Energy development—Environmental aspects—Juvenile literature. | Technological innovations—Juvenile literature. | Renewable energy sources—Juvenile literature.
Classification: LCC TJ163.23 E547 2020 | DDC 621.042—dc23

Manufactured in the United States of America

On the cover: A 3-D drilling simulator, an advanced tool to teach students at the Saudi Aramco Upstream Professional Development Center in Dharhan, Saudi Arabia, Jan. 10, 2018; Christophe Viseux/The New York Times.

Contents

CHAPTER 6

The Future: Energy and Policy Innovations

Introduction

THE SUN IS the origin of all the energy trapped on Earth in various forms: heat, matter, wind and motion. From the beginning, the story of human society and industry has been the ever more efficient and powerful harnessing of energy technology. Energy is possibility. In the form of fossil fuels — petroleum, coal and its variants — energy technologies such as the internal combustion engine drove the Industrial Revolution. Nuclear energy has shaped the planet both economically and politically, creating a singular world order of nuclear armed nations and at the same time producing relatively safe — in the short term, at least — and cheap electricity.

But the dream has always been to harness the forces of the sun itself, whether through some kind of controlled nuclear fusion reaction, mimicking the stars themselves, or more practically through technologies that collect and convert sunlight, heat and wind into useful electrical current. These solar-based systems are "sustainable" and "renewable," two terms one might read often in a discussion of energy and that speak to the heart of the urgency of this issue.

Since the Industrial Revolution and the dawn of mass production, on average, life has gotten better for human beings as a species, but growth has led to widespread pollution and the destruction of natural resources. Once oil or coal is extracted and burned for fuel, it becomes part of a chain of events that we now call global warming, or more broadly, climate change. Fossil fuels are unsustainable; in the end, at the scale with which we are deploying them, they will ruin the planet. Nuclear fuels are expensive and a security threat, and they contribute to pollution problems over the long term. We need a solar-based alternative as soon as possible.

DAMON WINTER/THE NEW YORK TIMES

Seen in reflection, Duke Energy's "Top of the World" wind farm near Glenrock, Wyo., Sept. 15, 2017. Four large wind farms have been built in recent years, and expansions are on the way.

While this argument might seem relatively straightforward, the politics of energy are complex and heated, especially in the United States, where energy production is linked to different cultural and social traditions: the generations of coal miners who see their way of life dying out, the families whose houses happen to sit on millions of dollars worth of shale gas ready for extraction, the communities in Alaska who either want to profit from oil drilling or believe it will destroy the state's valuable wilderness.

Americans have faced an array of tricky questions regarding energy and its production: Should we buy oil from our political rivals, thereby enriching them and making us beholden to them? How far are we willing to go to get cheap sources of energy? Far enough to join a war? How important is the environment weighed against social, political and economic strength? There are no easy answers.

The following pages contain an array of energy stories — about nuclear fission, oil extraction and pollution, the hunt for efficient solar energy, wind and geothermal technologies and more. Each of these stories has unique implications for the future of energy use, but they all intersect in their impact on climate change and the reality the human species will face in the future.

CHAPTER 1

The Long Dream of Clean Energy

It may be surprising to learn that engineers and scientists have been dreaming about harnessing solar energy for centuries. At each stage of development, from early mechanical engineering efforts to modern solar energy infrastructure, the dream of cheap, clean energy has connected with political and social goals: to avoid war over scarce resources, to allow everyone to live a high-quality life and to use the vast renewable power at our disposal to create new and innovative technologies that will improve life on Earth. In these articles, the sense of excitement and promise is palpable. But so too is the sense of urgency, especially in the 21st century, when industrial-fueled climate change is taking full effect and clean energy solutions have become more necessary.

New Solar Engine Gives Cheap Power

BY WILLIAM L. LAURENCE | DEC. 30, 1935

ST. LOUIS, DEC. 29. — The most efficient apparatus so far developed by man for the direct conversion of the rays of the sun into useful mechanical energy was demonstrated here today at the scientific exhibit of the American Association for the Advancement of Science, which opens its annual Winter meeting tomorrow.

The latest model of the solar engine makes another dream of science a practical reality. It was developed and displayed here by Dr. C. G. Abbott, secretary of the Smithsonian Institution, Washington, who has devoted many years of his life to efforts to devise means for harnessing the sun's limitless energy for the use of man.

His latest "sun-trap," Dr. Abbott said, constitutes a vast advance over the model he displayed last year. So efficient is it, he stated, that it is merely a question of comparative cost whether it should be used immediately for practical purposes.

As far as the apparatus is concerned, he added, the problem of converting solar radiation into useful energy has at last been solved.

CITES INEXHAUSTIBLE POWER.

"The means are available right now," he went on, "power from the sun in inexhaustible amounts, and all parts of the earth. It is merely a question of cost — whether it can be obtained as cheaply as power from coal, oil and gas."

The engine, he stated, utilizes fully 15 per cent of the energy of sunlight that falls on the surface of its parabolic mirror. The amount of energy obtained depends on the size of the mirror, which reflects 82 per cent of the light that falls on its surface.

This is four times the efficiency of any previous device for harnessing solar energy, Dr. Abbott asserted. A mirror containing seventy-two square feet would gather enough solar radiation for the production of 1 horsepower. A mirror of 7,200 square inches, which would be less than ninety feet per side, would produce 100 horsepower.

An area the size of the artificial lake created by Boulder Dam, if covered with similar parabolic mirrors, Dr. Abbott figured, would catch enough sunlight to produce 5,000,000 horsepower.

MIRROR OF ALUMINUM ALLOY.

The working model displayed by Dr. Abbott comprises an aluminum alloy mirror of parabolic cylindrical curvature 2 feet by 68 inches which focuses parallel rays of light on a vacuum-jacketed heater tube.

Within the tube, designed on the principle of the thermos bottle, is an opaque liquid, which can stand temperatures as high as 350 degrees Centigrade without boiling or flashing.

The available solar heat is absorbed by the opaque liquid and becomes concentrated to a degree sufficient to heat water within a reservoir which consists of a multiple-tube boiler.

From solar experiments, Dr. Abbott announced, "it is computed at a suitable outfit of this type can convert 15 per cent of intercepted solar energy into mechanical work through a steam engine."

The most efficient triple-expansion engine, Dr. Abbott pointed out, converts at best only 30 per cent of the energy contained in the coal it uses. The gasoline engine utilizes at most 35 per cent of the energy contained in the gasoline. A diesel engine and a mercury vapor boiler converted as high as 40 per cent of the fuel used into useful energy.

SOURCE COST IS NIL.

However, Dr. Abbott added, coal, gasoline and fuel oil cost money and are available in limited supplies, whereas solar energy is inexhaustible and costs nothing.

The only expense entailed in the solar engine, he added, is the initial cost of installation. Unlike silver, which has a reflecting power of 90 per cent of the light that falls upon it, but which tarnishes and would therefore require cleaning, the aluminum alloy does not tarnish, and, since the only work it would do would be to reflect light, it would practically last forever.

Similarly, he said, the black liquid circulating within the inner vacuum-jacketed tube will evaporate very little, if at all, in the course of time.

The only major difficulty, he declared, is the unavailability of sunlight at night and during cloudy days. This problem could be solved in a number of ways, he stated. The energy of the hours of sunlight could be stored up in huge storage batteries, or by making the sunlight energy pump water uphill, thus storing energy to be used when no sunlight is available.

Recent developments which make possible the transmission of electric power over great distances, Dr. Abbott added, open the vista for man of utilizing the desert areas on the world's continents, where the hot rays of the sun pour down endless amounts of energy in the form of sunlight every day, for vast sunlight power stations, whence power could be distributed to civilized areas of the globe.

The great deserts of Arizona and California could supply solar energy for the United States. The Sahara and desert spaces in Europe could supply enough sunlight-energy for the continent of Europe. Asia could get at sunlight power from the deserts of China, India and Arabia. Australia and Africa could utilize their deserts.

A Limitless Resource: Solar Energy

BY FARRINGTON DANIELS | MARCH 18, 1956

In a world that needs more and more power, intensive research goes forward on methods of 'harnessing' the sun.

SUNSHINE IS PERHAPS our most potent natural resource. Man has been using this solar energy ever since he has been man. He eats food that is the result of the sun's action in growing plants, whether he eats the vegetation itself or animals which have fed upon the vegetation. When he burns wood he is releasing the sun's energy which was stored up by chemical reaction in the growing tree.

In all civilizations solar energy is used directly in agriculture for growing food. It is also used directly for warmth. The Chinese build their courtyard walls to trap the warmth in a sunlit corner. The Japanese slide open the whole south side of the house to let in warming sun by day. Our architects use window walls in a similar manner. The Romans had solaria where people lay in the sun for the improvement of health.

In our civilization today we use solar energy indirectly on an enormous scale to do our work for us. Wood supplied sufficient fuels for a pioneer society, but it is utterly inadequate to supply our present needs. The typical fuel of the industrial revolution was coal. Today we add natural gas and oil. These familiar and abundant "fossil fuels" — coal, gas and oil — came from vegetable material produced by sunlight millions of years ago and buried by geological accidents.

These fuels operate our machines, our automobiles and trains and our planes. They heat our homes and offices, run our furnaces and factories. They produce most of our electricity. Even the electricity obtained from water power comes indirectly from solar energy, for it is the warmth of the sun that evaporates from sea and land the water which rises as vapor, falls as rain and flows in rivers to give us hydroelectric power at every waterfall and dam.

ALL OVER THE WORLD there is a clamor for more energy. Scientists in many lands are making a concentrated effort toward finding ways of putting the sun's energy to work more directly, more efficiently and on a much broader scale. Just recently a conference on Applied Solar Energy was held in Arizona which brought together a thousand scientists, engineers and observers, including eighty-six scientists from abroad. In 1954 a similar meeting was held in India and in 1953 one at the University of Wisconsin. It is evident that solar energy is now commanding not only academic but practical and official interest on a wide front.

There are two different ways of using the sun's energy. The sun itself is a huge incandescent ball, kept at temperatures of a million degrees and more by atomic or nuclear reactions. Its radiation spreads out in all directions and our earth is in line with only a tiny fraction of it. Of the radiation coming our way only a part gets through the atmosphere and the clouds and reaches the surface of the earth.

About half the radiation which the earth receives is in the form of visible light which can bring about chemical reactions, and the other half, which cannot be seen by the human eye, is chemically inactive but gives radiant heat. Both forms, the light and the radiant heat, can be used for heating and for operating engines.

The most common action of the visible light is that of photosynthesis — literally "putting together by means of light." In this remarkable process of nature for growing plants, carbon dioxide of the air is combined with water by light in the presence of green chlorophyll. The result is sugar and other plant materials. We use these plant materials as food and fuel and fibers. But the use of invisible light, the radiant heat for operating engines, is in its infancy.

Why are we becoming so interested in inventing solar engines? Coal, gas and oil are abundant in the United States and our present engines were created to use these fuels. Atomic energy seems to be within reach. Do we need to develop any other energy resources?

We are coming to realize that our fossil fuels will not always be abundant. In the long run they will be exhausted — natural gas first, oil next, and finally coal. Even now, coal shortages are imminent in parts of Europe. Though new oil potentials are being discovered, old ones are being drained and are irreplaceable.

Atomic energy offers great hopes, but it has its limitations. It can come only in large million-dollar packages and it has problems of disposal of radioactive wastes. Solar energy, on the other hand, can be useful in small, inexpensive units. Both these sources of energy are weightless and so, unlike coal and oil, they do no require costly transportation to the place where they are to be used.

THE URANIUM WHICH supplies atomic energy is abundant and will last longer than our oil and coal but, like them, it is eventually an irreplaceable resource. Energy from the sun, however, is being constantly renewed and it is more abundant than any conceivable need of man, and there is no prospect of its diminishing within millions of years.

At present, in industrialized countries, the use of solar energy will not offer competition to coal and oil and electrical power, but solar power may well compete with the manpower and the animal power used in nonindustrialized countries.

Accordingly, it is important that we investigate to the fullest the possibilities of power from the sun, because economic progress depends upon an assured and expanding supply of power. Already we are aware that underdeveloped areas in many parts of the world need greater resources of low-cost power in order to take their places among the productive and prosperous communities. They need power to pump water for irrigation and sanitation, power to provide manufactured goods, power to provide amenities of living. They need solar energy now, and other areas will need it when their fossil fuels are depleted.

Many interesting applications of solar energy have already been made but as yet they are not wholly practical. Most of them have centered on various means of concentrating the diffuse and gentle rays of the sun. A high temperature is needed to convert heat into useful work. The burning glass — a lens that focuses the rays to a point — is familiar.

IN 1884, IN Paris, an experimental printing press was shown in which sunlight, concentrated by mirrors, operated a steam engine. For a time, in 1913, a twenty-horse-power "sun engine" pumped water from the Nile. More recently, temperatures up to 5,500 degrees Fahrenheit have been obtained for experimental purposes by focusing large and perfect mirrors. A few experimental houses have been heated by sunlight falling on the roof. India has produced small solar cookers. But no generally applicable success has yet been attained in any of these fields.

The reasons are several. Large and perfect parabolic mirrors are expensive to make; their surfaces collect dust, which cuts their efficiency and has to be removed; they require machinery to turn them so that they will always center on the moving sun. In solar house-heating, materials and construction methods are more costly at present than those of conventional methods.

Theoretically, however, there is sufficient incentive to encourage the use of solar energy. For example, in bright sunlight the roof of a house receives in a day a quantity of heat which is equivalent to a man's weight in coal or a to a small automobile tankful of gasoline. It may be possible to convert this into about 50 kilowatt-hours of electricity. These opportunities will be of less interest in New York and other cities than in areas of the world where there are fewer people to every acre of sunshine.

INTENSIVE RESEARCH is going forward along five well-defined avenues. They are:

(1) Collecting and concentrating. The mirrors hitherto used to gather and focus rays have been mostly of glass, and costly for general use. Now work is being done on aluminum foil and aluminized plastic sheets molded in parabolic form.

Another method of collection employs multiple plates of plain glass placed over a blacklined box containing water or other liquids. Radiation enters through the glass and heats the interior but the heat cannot escape and so it accumulates. The heated fluid can be piped away for use. Here the difficulty so far has been building cheap accumulators large enough to develop significant quantities of heat.

(2) Solar Engines. These are devices aimed at generating steam in such pressure and quantity as to produce mechanical power (e.g., to drive a pump for irrigation). One design has a long semi-cylindrical parabolic mirror at the focus of which is an iron pipe containing water and enclosed in a glass tube which traps the heat. The steam is produced in the pipe and conducted away for use. A similar machine uses liquids such as sulfur dioxides, which boil at lower temperatures than water.

(3) Solar House-Heating. This represents a technically easier operation than the generation of steam because the temperatures required are lower. The methods range from simply installing a large window wall facing south (to give supplementary heat) to installing large collectors on the roof for heating water which circulates through pipes and radiators. Solar refrigeration and air-conditioning are technically possible also.

MUCH THE SAME principle is involved in the technique of evaporating sea water to get fresh water. A glass or plastic roof, slightly tilted, catches the rising vapor, condenses it and allows it to run down to a collecting trough.

(4) Photochemistry. Here, man is trying to duplicate what plants do all by themselves — using sunlight to bring about a chemical change, with the absorption of energy. This energy is "stored" and it can be made available whenever needed by releasing it in another chemical reaction. For example, when water is separated into oxygen and hydrogen, latent energy is stored in the gases. When they are reunited the equivalent in heat is given off. It is theoretically possible to carry on this kind of process by photochemistry, but no one has yet found just the right substances to make it work. The fact that nature already does this on an enormous scale should be a pacesetter and a challenge to our young scientists.

(5) Photoelectricity. This is the newest and in some ways the most exciting of the prospects that are open. Here sunlight is converted directly into electricity. Light falling on certain kinds of crystals generates current, without consuming any material. In bright sunlight a batter of these crystals will produce electricity at the rate of nearly 100 watts per square yard of exposed surface, amounting to a 10 per cent conversion of the sunlight's power into electricity. Not long ago, installations of this kind provided enough power to operate a rural telephone circuit and a small radio transmitter.

IN ALL THESE fields one elemental difficulty prevails: the sun doesn't shine all the time. There are the hours of nighttime darkness and the days of heavy clouds. This means that for most purposes a practical and economical means of storing either the heat or the energy must be found. Already it can be done technically in various ways. For instance, a solar steam engine can drive an electric generator to charge storage batteries, which can then be tapped as needed. But these batteries are expensive, and not effective for prolonged use. A cheaper and perhaps different kind of battery must be found.

Heat received during the hours of sunlight can be stored up in water, in certain chemicals or even in enclosed beds upon hours of darkness. But large quantities are needed and this presents engineering, economic and architectural problems.

An indirect method of storing the sun's energy is in the creation of food and fuel. Agriculture uses this process all the time but, technically, the efficiency of this conversion is not high. Only a small fraction of 1 per cent of the year's solar energy which falls on the land is stored in an average corn crop or forest. In the mass culture of green algae, a conversion of as much as 10 per cent is possible. But here again the cost of apparatus is very high. In the laboratory, under the most favorable conditions, 30 per cent of the light actually absorbed can be stored by growing algae.

The possibilities and the difficulties in the use of solar energy pose a challenge to scientists. They also pose a challenge to governments. There is today an obvious imbalance in the world's basic economy, and that imbalance involves the availability and use of energy.

The industrialized areas, chiefly North America and Europe, use 82 per cent of all the effective energy used in the world. Because we have abundant fuels and abundant initiative and freedom, plus education and research, we have developed a mechanized civilization that gives the highest material standard of living ever known. On the average, every one of us feeds himself food equivalent to 3,000 kilocalories a day but in the same period feeds his machines the equivalent of 164,000 kilocalories.

This quantity of energy is not at present available to much of the rest of the world. And the rest of the world is stirring in its knowledge of and desire for similar abundance. Yet, efforts in solar research have thus far been small and the problems are many. Some work has been backed by the Cabot Foundation at the Massachusetts Institute of Technology and Harvard; by the Kettering Foundation at Yellow Springs, Ohio; by the Guggenheim Foundation, and on a larger scale by the Rockefeller Foundation at the University of Wisconsin.

Government laboratories of India, Russia and the United States Department of the Interior have carried on some research. It seems strange that although our own Government has spent billions of dollars for atomic energy and for agriculture, it has spend only thousands for direct research on solar energy. Yet solar energy is far greater in potential supply and it involves no need for secrecy, no environmental hazard, and no large capital investment in pilot plants.

IT MUST BE EMPHASIZED that no new era of solar energy prosperity is just around the corner. Years of research and development are necessary.

But the basic conceptions are in our grasp and without much doubt can be brought to realization.

For the world as a whole, the outlook in sources of energy is good. In this latter half of the twentieth century a judicious use of fossil fuels in conventional ways, atomic energy in large units near cities, and solar energy in rural areas should provide all the energy that is needed anywhere.

This next age of abundant power may tend to equalize industrial and economic opportunities and relieve tensions that might lead to war. It is well, however, to remember that "man does no live by kilowatts alone," and other world problems need also to be solved.

FARRINGTON DANIELS, the chairman of the Department of Chemistry at the University of Wisconsin, is recognized as the leading authority on solar energy in this country.

U.S. Harnessing Volcanic Steam

BY KATHLEEN MCLAUGHLIN | OCT. 21, 1962

UNITED NATIONS, N.Y. — Next March, the only geothermal power plant in the United States is expected to be generating 25,000 kilowatts of electricity, twice its present capacity.

The plant, which has been operating since the summer of 1960 in Big Sulphur Canyon near Cloverdale, Calif., produces electricity from steam that is captured from the underground geysers at the site and funneled into regular steam turbines for power production.

Constructed by the Pacific Gas and Electric Company of San Francisco at a cost of $2,000,000, the first unit has proved very successful, according to Albert L. Bruce, chief engineer. The second unit will use steam from the same field.

The power generated is distributed through the same grid as that from conventional plants and has proved about equally inexpensive.

LIMIT IS AUTOMATIC

The Geysers Power Plant, as it is known, is entirely automatic in operation, requiring no staff. It depends on an alarm system to alert the manned Fulton Substation about any interruption in service. It was the world's first privately-finanaced geothermal plant.

Presently the extension of electric power from other subterranean steam sources is in prospect, the Geothermal Energy Corporation having contracted for a 15,000-kilowatt plant — Casa Diablo Hot Springs — to be built at the site 45 miles north of Bishop, Calif. It is scheduled for opening in 1964 and will sell power to the California Power Company in the region around San Bernardino.

At Beowawe in Nevada, near Elko, the Magma Power Company has drilled four wells and is negotiating with utilities in the area for another geothermal power station.

FURTHER STUDIES UNDER WAY

Two other drillings by Geothermal, Inc., at Calipatria in the Imperial Valley and at O'Neill, near Fresno, Calif., have reached 5,000 feet and obtained water vapor at 530 degrees Fahrenheit, but with 35 per cent salt infusion. Studies are under way to determine the feasibility of their economic exploitation.

Comparable activities in many other nations reflect developments since the United Nations sponsored a conference on this and other new sources of energy, at the Rome headquarters of the Food and Agriculture Organization. Participants inspected Italy's pioneer geothermal plant at Lardarello, which has long produced low-cost electricity to power the nation's railways, as well as other industries.

New Zealand's enormous resources of steam of volcanic origin have been harnessed for industrial and other applications of the energy produced. Mexico, Guatemala and Japan particularly are working toward the same objective.

Earlier this year, Iceland obtained a $2,000,000 loan from the International Bank for Reconstruction and Development (World Bank), to help with a $5,600,000 program of extension of the mains through which Reyjavik, the capital, is heated by water from hot artesian wells. About 30 miles of pipe are being added to the system.

SOLAR ENERGY STUDIES

In the field of solar energy, the most extensive use of radiation continues to be for water heaters, already functioning in vast numbers in several countries. Japan has a long lead, with a total of 350,000 by the end of 1960, and a target of 1,000,000 to be in operation by 1965. Estimates are that more than 1,000,000 tons a year of high-cost fuel will represent the total savings at that time.

In the United States 25,000 such units are employed in Florida alone, and Israel, where conditions are optimal for them, is increasing her total of 10,000 in use last year.

While electric energy from the sun remains the chief objective of the experiments under way, equipment in present use is proving its value in a variety of tasks.

Solar drying of agricultural crops and other products has been employed in tropical countries particularly. Solar stoves for cooking have had some limited use, but production costs have not yet been reduced to the level they must reach for wide adoption in developing areas where they are most needed.

Meeting the Energy Dilemma

EDITORIAL | BY THE NEW YORK TIMES | JULY 20, 1971

THE BASIC ENERGY DILEMMA of modern society is by now well understood. To provide rising standards of living to increasing populations here and abroad, more energy of all types must be available. But virtually all present major modes of energy generation impose costs upon the environment; automobile exhausts spew noxious gases into the atmosphere; nuclear fission reactors produce thermal pollution and long-lasting radioactive substances as waste byproducts. In all industrialized countries men are debating how far their nations dare go in fouling air, water and soil to satisfy the present insatiable demand for more power. Everyone now recognizes that there are limits to the volume of effluent the planetary environment can absorb and still continue to permit the survival of plant and animal life.

There is even a rising skepticism in some quarters about the desirability of further economic growth. Traditionally production growth has been looked to as the source of increased wealth and a ceiling on production would therefore threaten society with social, economic and political struggles over the redistribution of a fixed and inadequate annual national income.

A way out of the energy dilemma, however, may lie in the development of power sources which exact minimum environmental costs or none at all. Two possibilities stand out in this regard. One is development of controlled thermonuclear fusion — a tamed version of the hydrogen bomb — as a major source of electricity, a source that might have many fewer environmental costs and drawbacks than any of the nuclear fission techniques now either being employed or developed. A second possibility is a new and far more sophisticated approach to the exploitation of solar energy. Under this proposal, "power satellites" would be sent into space to absorb solar energy and transmit it to earth in microwave form which could then be turned into electricity.

A variant is the Soviet idea of setting up stations on the moon for collecting solar energy and transmitting it to earth via microwave from that natural satellite.

President Nixon has given evidence that he is aware of the energy dilemma. He could move constructively to meet it by substantially increasing the amount now being spent on fusion power research and by initiating serious efforts to develop solar power plants in space or here on earth itself.

A 30-Year Plan for Pollution-Free Energy Sources

OPINION | BY LELAN F. SILLIN JR. | DEC. 13, 1971

HARTFORD — The goal: an electric power supply essential to man's harmonious relationship to his physical environment and necessary to his future social well-being. To achieve such a supply may require as much as thirty years of intense research effort. The search for such an energy supply should, therefore, be a central purpose for the electric utility industry and the nation over the next generation.

A road map is developing which suggests the course we are ultimately bound to follow in our pursuit of the elusive goal of abundant pollution-free energy sources. This road map suggests the use of nuclear power augmented by the "breeder" and other technology during the period of transition to a source based on fusion, solar energy or some other esoteric system.

The most important current power generation goal is the nuclear "breeder reactor." It would comprise the first of three steps in a proposed $40-billion, thirty-year program of research.

The second step would be geared to other areas of research having a high priority during the transitional period.

Within the 1972-90 period a number of major technological advances can be achieved if aggressively pursued. Before 1980, improvements to power generation technology may include fuel cells for use in substations, large high-energy batteries for peak loads, high temperature gas-cooled nuclear reactors, devices for removal of sulphur dioxide and nitrous oxide from power-plant flue gases and coal gasification.

Transmission advances in this period may include compressed gas insulated cable for underground transmission, higher voltage alternating current for improved overhead transmission and developments in direct current technology.

In the period prior to 1990 we might anticipate magnetohydrodynamics combined cycles; and in the transmission area, cryogenic underground transmission. These projects, together with additional technology to improve air and water quality and esthetics, suggest the range of requirements and opportunities. This portion of the program is estimated to require an annual industry commitment equivalent to approximately one-half of 1 per cent of annual revenues, and would be supplemented by an additional one-half of 1 per cent upon completion of the breeder program.

To accomplish this 1972-90 program, venture capital electric research firms should be established in six or seven regions of the United States.

The success of these research firms would be measured in the quality and level of response to critical environmental, social and technological issues. Industry participants would have to contribute more than money and talent.

The third step of the proposed research program is the development of the virtually pollution-free power system, perhaps utilizing fusion or solar power as the source, and super-conductive underground cable, microwave or some other advanced concept for transmission.

The development of such a system can be a rallying point, a restorer of confidence — even a unifying national goal. I call it a project for Prometheus.

This system has such importance and such a different time dimension that it should be pursued by a separate and a political entity — perhaps a public-private arrangement after the image of Comsat. As always, the problem is how to begin. A panel of experts from among the industry, as well as from such groups as the National Academy of Sciences, National Academy of Engineering, American Bar Association, Office of Science and Technology, Council on Environmental Quality and representatives of state and Federal regulatory authorities, should flesh out the plan and test the validity of scientific, technological, financial and organizational objectives.

Various authors have described the social world toward which we are moving as the "post industrial" era, that time in the evolution of developed nations when, through advancing technology, production capacity outstrips consumption needs.

Society could choose to use this excess capacity to engage in large scale national programs, such as extensive city rebuilding, transportation renovation, restoration of the environment, further space exploration, and so on. It might elect to take a portion of this excess capacity in the form of leisure, with increasing participation in education and the arts. In short, the proposition for Project Prometheus: If society does those things today to encourage planning ahead for the essential energy sources, it enhances the prospects of plenty and dignity for future generations.

LELAN F. SILLIN JR. is chairman and president of Northeast Utilities in Hartford.

In Hurricane Harvey's Wake, We Need a Green 'New Deal'

OPINION | BY REBECCA ELLIOTT | AUG. 31, 2017

FOR ALL OF the uncertainties that await Houston and coastal Texas, we can be reasonably sure about one thing: Many of those flooded out by Hurricane Harvey will watch their investments and savings collapse into debt and bankruptcy. And the heaviest burdens, of course, will fall on the shoulders of low- and middle-income residents.

Preliminary estimates put losses from the storm at $30 billion to $40 billion. If past disasters are any indication, those numbers will only grow in the coming days and weeks. Whatever the ultimate figure, the losses will represent, in part, the aggregation of hundreds of thousands or more individual financial calamities. When the waters recede and Houstonians and others hit by this storm return home, with all their pluck and determination, to muck out and clear debris, many will learn too late that their homeowners' insurance does not cover flood damage.

Even for the lucky 15 percent of homeowners in Houston and surrounding Harris County, who have a federal flood policy in place, collecting claims will most likely be a protracted and contentious process. (Hurricane Katrina and Sandy victims have stories to tell about fraudulent or erroneous claims adjustments, delayed payments and their homes being unlivable for years.) Many of the other 85 percent were not required to have a flood policy because they were not officially at "high risk" on the region's flood maps — maps that President Trump no longer wants the government to pay for.

Those homeowners will be forced to fall back on some combination of disaster relief, loans and savings. Although homeowners with government-backed mortgages will be able to hold off on payments for at least 90 days, eventually they will have to honor mortgages on

ILANA PANICH-LINSMAN FOR THE NEW YORK TIMES

People in Spring, Tex., waiting to be ferried to their flooded homes to collect their belongings.

houses that are uninhabitable or even swept away. Renters may never return home.

In short, many Texans will be starting over economically.

As the legal scholar Michele Dauber has shown, President Franklin D. Roosevelt understood the relationship between "ruined landscapes and ruined lives." Roosevelt likened the Great Depression to the devastation of the Dust Bowl, tornadoes in Georgia, and floods on the Mississippi and Ohio Rivers to build his case for the huge public investments and assistance programs that transformed the fates of Americans who were also starting over.

In the last several decades of American policy making, however, we have seen those protections and provisions eroded, along with divestments in the kinds of public goods like knowledge and infrastructure that help us to live safe and secure lives, in good times and bad. The outpouring of solidarity and support we have seen from ordinary people during Hurricane Harvey is not matched by programs that institutionalize a commitment to collective flourishing. This has been for many Americans its own kind of slow-motion disaster.

A recent report by American scientists concluded that the effects of climate change are already with us. In a world of more Harveys, rising sea levels, heat waves and droughts, what do we owe each other? The political trajectory we have been on suggests that the answer is, "Very little."

Congress and state legislatures disburse emergency funds, which are then offset in budgets with cuts to social services and public spending. We are seemingly in a permanently reactive mode, with money often going to rebuild "back to normal" as though this is proof of bravery in the face of tremendous uncertainty. Recovery from previous disasters, like Hurricane Katrina, has had regressive effects, heightening the disparities between rich and poor and perpetuating systemic racism.

Certainly, the hurricane's victims need all the help we can provide. But this historic storm, like the Great Depression, should also motivate a reconsideration of our broader social contract: a new New Deal.

Environmentalists and scholars have sometimes called this a "green New Deal" or "environmental Keynesianism." We should invest in science and public education to train the next generation of engineers who will build safer homes and infrastructure. (President Trump promised us infrastructure but, just weeks before this storm, rescinded an Obama-era regulation that required structures built with federal money to take sea-level rise into account.) We should expand and enhance programs that make adaptation to climate change possible for ordinary Americans, helping them to retrofit their homes or relocate to safer ground.

We should plan recovery and rebuilding projects that address local poverty and exclusion, rather than line the pockets of developers. We should commit expenditures to the kinds of projects that mitigate climate change, like clean energy and public transportation. And we should strengthen our safety nets so that when the next storm's victims are picking up the pieces, they are not also worried about job insecurity, rising health care costs and precarious retirements.

How we respond to Hurricane Harvey and the floods to come will demonstrate who and what we value. We care for one another — that much is clear from the rescue efforts. A new New Deal commits us to caring for one another after the disaster has passed.

REBECCA ELLIOTT is an assistant professor of sociology at the London School of Economics.

The Green New Deal Rises Again

OPINION | BY THOMAS L. FRIEDMAN | JAN. 8, 2019

It was a good idea that didn't catch on in 2007. Now we're running out of time.

BACK IN 2007, I wrote a column calling for a "Green New Deal," and I later expanded on the idea in a book, "Hot, Flat and Crowded." Barack Obama picked up the theme and made a Green New Deal part of his 2008 platform, but the idea just never took off. So I'm excited that the new Democratic Congresswoman Alexandria Ocasio-Cortez and others have put forward their own takes on a Green New Deal, and it's now getting some real attention.

There is no agreed-upon policy road map for a Green New Deal. But as one of the leading climate bloggers, Joe Romm, recently pointed out, "Since the midterms, dozens of U.S. representatives and at least four Democratic senators have pledged support to create a Select Committee to create legislation for a Green New Deal. The goal is a 'detailed national, industrial, economic mobilization plan' to rapidly transition the country away from fossil fuels and toward clean energy, such as a solar, wind, and electric cars."

The Green New Deal that Ocasio-Cortez has laid out aspires to power the U.S. economy with 100 percent renewable energy within 12 years and calls for "a job guarantee program to assure a living wage job to every person who wants one," "basic income programs" and "universal health care," financed, at least in part, by higher taxes on the wealthy. Critics argue that this is technically unfeasible and that combining it with democratic socialist proposals will drive off conservatives needed to pass it.

Myself, I like the urgency and energy she and groups like the Sunrise Movement are bringing to this task. So for now I say: Let a hundred Green New Deal ideas bloom! Let's see what sticks and what falls by the wayside.

My own definition of a Green New Deal, which has evolved since 2007 as the technology has gotten better and the climate problem has gotten worse, remains focused on how a green revolution in America can drive innovation, spur new industries and enhance our security. Originally I also thought it could help us get our groove back after the 2007-8 recession. Success required changes in attitude, scale and innovation.

Clean energy is a problem of scale. If you don't have scale, you have a hobby. I like hobbies. I used to build model airplanes. But you can't mitigate climate change as a hobby. The reason I called for a Green New Deal was first and foremost to convey that this undertaking required a massive, urgent response commensurate with the scale and time frame posed by accelerating disruptive climate.

For too long "green" was viewed as a synonym for a project that was boutique, uneconomical, liberal, sissy and vaguely French. I wanted to recast green as geostrategic, capitalistic, economical, innovative and patriotic. My motto was, "Green is the new red, white and blue." I did not believe in being a "nice" green. I believed in being a mean green. I believed greens should be as brassy, bold, big sky and in-your-face as any oil and gas executive.

I liked the way environmental writer David Roberts put it in 2008: "Like so much of the American left, the environmental movement has become acclimated to the notion that it is operating outside the mainstream, knocking sheepishly on the door. Its rallying cry might as well be, 'If it's not too much trouble. ...' " Forget that, Roberts argued, it is time for the green movement to think big and make big demands — something oil and gas executives do every day.

To achieve scale, though, my view was that a Green New Deal had to be embraced by more than liberals. You had to reach conservatives and even climate deniers. My way of doing that was to focus on something we can all agree on: math. There are about 7.6 billion people on the planet today and, according to the United Nations, there will be 8.6 billion in 2030. A *billion* more people driving, flying, eating protein, building homes and drinking water in just over a decade.

If they all adopt the per-capita consumption habits of today's Americans, we're going to burn up, heat up, eat up, plow up, choke up and smoke up the planet, whether the climate changes or not. That means that clean power, clean cars, clean manufacturing, clean water and energy efficiency have to be the next great global industries — otherwise, we humans are going to be a bad biological experiment, whether the climate changes or not.

Who believes that America can remain a great country and not lead the next great global industry? Not me. A Green New Deal, in other words, is a strategy for American national security, national resilience, natural security and economic leadership in the 21st century. Surely some conservatives can support that.

And to make sure that they have an incentive to, I would also guarantee that a portion of every dollar raised by a carbon tax in a Green New Deal would be invested in two new community colleges and high-speed broadband in rural areas of every state. Each state could decide where. Every American needs to feel a chance to gain from a Green New Deal.

But which Green New Deal? Mine is focused on innovation. I believe there is only one thing as big as Mother Nature, and that is Father Greed — a.k.a., the market. I am a green capitalist. I think we will only get the scale we need by shaping the market. If I were drafting a Green New Deal platform today, it would put in place steadily rising mileage, manufacturing and emissions standards; stronger building codes; and carbon market prices that would say to our industries and innovators: Here are the goals, here is the level of clean power or efficiency that you have to hit every year — and may the best company win.

As I wrote in my 2007 column: "To spark a Green New Deal today requires getting two things right: government regulations and prices. Look at California. By setting steadily higher standards for the energy efficiency of buildings and appliances — and creating incentives for utilities to work with consumers to use less power — California has held its per-capita electricity use constant for 30 years, while the rest of the nation has seen per-capita electricity use increase by nearly 50 percent, according to the Natural Resources Defense Council. That has saved California from building 24 giant power plants."

To keep it simple, my goals would be what energy innovator Hal Harvey has dubbed "the four zeros." 1. Zero-net energy buildings: buildings that can produce as much energy as they consume. 2. Zero-waste manufacturing: stimulating manufacturers to design and build products that use fewer raw materials and that are easily disassembled and recycled. 3. A zero-carbon grid: If we can combine renewable power generation at a utility scale with some consumers putting up their own solar panels and windmills that are integrated with the grid, and with large-scale storage batteries, we really could, one day, electrify everything carbon-free. 4. Zero-emissions transportation: a result of combining electric vehicles and electric public transportation with a zero-carbon grid.

That's my Green New Deal circa 2019. It basically says: Forget the Space Race. We don't need a man, or woman, on Mars. We need an Earth Race — a free-market competition to ensure that mankind can continue to thrive on Earth. A Green New Deal is the strategy for that. It can make America healthier, wealthier, more innovative, more energy secure, more respected — and weaken petro-dictators across the globe.

I am eager to see what other people propose, but we don't have another decade to waste. This may well be our last chance to build the technologies we need at the scale of the challenge we face in the time we still have to — as scientists say — manage the unavoidable aspects of climate change and avoid the unmanageable ones.

As the environmentalist Dana Meadows once put it, "We have exactly enough time — starting now."

THOMAS L. FRIEDMAN is the foreign affairs Op-Ed columnist. He joined the paper in 1981, and has won three Pulitzer Prizes. He is the author of seven books, including "From Beirut to Jerusalem," which won the National Book Award.

We Need More Than Solar and Wind to Power the Green New Deal

OPINION | BY JESSE JENKINS AND SAMUEL THERNSTROM | JAN. 17, 2019

We're also going to need nuclear, geothermal and fossil-fuel plants that capture and store their emissions.

SINCE THE EARLY DAYS of the modern environmental movement, activists have embraced solar and wind power. A "small is beautiful" mantra guided a "soft path" to the renewables revolution.

That vision inspired an open letter sent last week by hundreds of grass-roots environmental groups to Congress demanding a rapid transition to 100 percent renewable energy and explicitly rejecting virtually all forms of emissions-free power except solar and wind. The letter (notably lacking the signatures of six of the major national environmental groups) is one of several competing efforts to define a Green New Deal, an inchoate idea that has recently captured the political imagination on the center and left.

The energy and ambition of this effort is certainly worthy of applause. But environmental leaders in Congress must recognize a hard truth. The Green New Deal will be no deal if all it buys us is solar and wind power.

A breakthrough on climate will depend on a willingness by Democrats and others to harness the well-intended ambition of activists while focusing on practical ways to take carbon out of our power system. Otherwise, Republicans won't go along, and it won't be feasible for the electric power grid.

Wind and solar have come a long way since the early days. These sources now produce about 9 percent of the electricity in the United States, and their costs have declined dramatically in recent years.

We can celebrate that progress without turning it into a narrow mandate. We recently reviewed 40 studies of decarbonization pathways, and the results could not have been clearer. Without exception, every study that sought to identify the most affordable clean electricity system without artificially constraining available technology options reached the same conclusion: It was much cheaper to include so-called firm low-carbon technologies such as nuclear, carbon capture, or reliable but often overlooked renewables like geothermal or hydro dams with large reservoirs, than it would be to build a clean energy system without them.

Firm electricity generation resources are available on demand, for any length of time, any season of the year. That makes them a critical complement to weather-dependent wind and solar, as well as resources like batteries or strategies like demand flexibility (which permits consumers to reduce their electricity use in periods when supplies are strained) that are best suited to fast bursts of use.

In other words, firm technologies complete the clean energy team. Wind and solar add value to the grid and can even be star players. But they aren't cut out to win the decarbonization game all on their own.

Why? The variability challenge of renewables is greater than is generally appreciated. The problem is not simply the setting sun and the hourly dips in wind generation; the toughest challenge comes from the weeks and months when wind and solar production decline dramatically because of seasonal factors or prolonged weather fronts.

To get through those lengthy periods, renewables-dominated systems have to be supersized, installing three to eight times more power capacity than peak demand so they can fill the void when solar and wind output is diminished. That means they also produce way too much electricity when favorable conditions return. That excess is either wasted or stored (at a cost) for later use. And, presently, storage technologies are not available to do the job cost effectively at the scale we are talking about. If such a system were to be built, it would feature a lot of poorly utilized, capital-intensive wind, solar and storage assets. Unless the cost of those technologies falls to extremely low levels, we'll be forced to choose between clean energy and affordability. The recent riots in Paris show how that conflict might play out.

Clean power systems with a mix of fuels can more easily match generation to demand and productively use all assets more often, making these systems more economical to operate. There's no waste of large surpluses of energy or the need to develop seasonal energy storage. These advantages make the economics of a balanced low-carbon power system more attractive than those that rely solely on weather-dependent renewables. Maintaining fuel diversity also minimizes the zero-sum politics of an all-renewables grid. We don't need to shutter the nuclear and fossil fuel industries to achieve environmental goals.

To be clear, firm energy technologies face daunting challenges of their own. No one believes it is easy to build nuclear or carbon-capture power plants, which would capture carbon dioxide emissions and utilize or permanently store them. Enhanced geothermal energy (which uses techniques similar to fracking to unlock renewable energy) is still an emerging technology. But the value of these resources to a decarbonized power system would be very high, justifying efforts to accelerate their development and deployment.

We are not alone in our conclusions. In his State of the State address Tuesday, Gov. Andrew Cuomo of New York deliberately outlined a transition to a 100-percent clean, carbon-free energy system by 2040 — not an all-renewables system. California recently did the same. When two of the most environmentally progressive states both see the wisdom of a broad path to decarbonization, activists would be wise to heed their pragmatic conclusions.

Expanding and improving the set of firm, carbon-free energy resources would make it much more affordable and feasible to eliminate greenhouse gas emissions from electric power plants. That's something Green New Dealers and Americans of all political stripes could get behind.

JESSE JENKINS is a postdoctoral environmental fellow at Harvard.
SAMUEL THERNSTROM is the founder and executive director of the Energy Innovation Reform Project, and a senior fellow at the Center for the National Interest.

CHAPTER 2

Black Gold: Oil, Industry, Pollution and Conflict

Fossil fuels, which include oil, natural gas and coal, have constituted the bulk of energy resource consumption in the industrial era. Oil is highly efficient, can be transported by tankers or pipelines and is abundant — but not infinitely so. Aside from being nonrenewable, burning fossil fuels produces pollution, which contributes to climate change. The consequences of oil — having it, finding it, spilling it, burning it, buying and selling it — are far-reaching and critical for understanding the modern political world and the changes to come.

Power in Oil World Vastly Different Since 1967 War

BY WILLIAM D. SMITH | JUNE 6, 1972

THE SIX-DAY Arab-Israeli War, which began five years ago yesterday, set in motion forces that have sharply changed the international oil industry.

The changes are still occurring, as last week's nationalization of the Western-owned oil consortium by Iraqi's Government shows. In the last five years the oil industry has lost some of its physical strength as well as emotional drive.

The period since 1967 has seen the entrance of the Soviet Union as a major participant in Middle East political and petroleum affairs.

It also has seen a radical swing in the balance of negotiating power from the industrialized nations of the Western world (and Japan) to the oil-producing states.

During the same five years the United States, for the first time in its peacetime history, has faced the threat of energy supply difficulties and possible shortages. A solution for these energy problems is likely to have to come from the Middle East, where almost 70 per cent of the world's oil reserves lie.

'WINDS OF CHANGE'

In an article in Foreign Affairs, Walter Levy, the oil economist, remarked that "the winds of change have begun to blow through the world oil trade." In a subsequent speech, he amended this comment to say, "The winds of change have turned into a hurricane."

A major shift in the velocity of these winds occurred in 1967 when the Arabs accused the United States and other Western nations of siding with Israel.

During the six-day war the Arab nations cut off supplies to the Western oil companies: They quickly decided that this was counterproductive because the Arab cause needed money at least as much as the industrialized countries needed oil.

Nonetheless, there remained a substantial residue of ill will toward the Western companies.

SUEZ CANAL CLOSED

The war closed the Suez Canal, tightening the world's oil supply lines. Europe began counting more and more on Libya, just across the Mediterranean in North Africa, which now supplies almost 40 per cent of its oil.

A break in the Trans-Arabian pipelines in Syria further tightened oil supply lines, and the cost of tankers to carry oil rose sharply.

In the meantime, a 29-year-old militant Colonel, Muammar el-Qaddafi, had overthrown the monarchy in Libya.

He used the situation to ask for higher payments for Libyan oil, now vitally important to Europe. The oil companies initially responded with an offer he said was insulting, The revolutionary demanded sharply higher posted prices and tax payments.

The oil executives looked at the world supply situation and suddenly realized they were holding a weak hand. Colonel Qaddafi was just as surprised to discover that he, not the Western companies, held the trumps.

BIG GAINS ACHIEVED

The Libyans obtained a sharp increase in the posted price as well as an increase in the tax rate to 55 per cent from 50 per cent.

These gains did not go unnoticed by other oil-producing nations. Within months the other 10 members of the Organization of Petroleum Exporting Countries had negotiated similar agreements.

The oil companies, even though they banded together to face the OPEC demands, submitted almost entirely to the demands of the producing nations, The once powerful international oil industry was virtually helpless in the face of what amounted to a cartel of oil-producing nations.

"The oil trade became a seller's market for the first time in its modern peacetime history," Prof. Henry Adelman of M.I.T. commented.

FINANCIAL POWER

The price increases will amount to almost $10 billion for the oil-producing nations by 1975, when the present agreements were scheduled to run out. This money gives the producing nations considerable financial power, which is likely to increase as the years go by.

The contracts failed to survive one year. The OPEC demanded compensation for the devaluation of the dollar. It also called for 20 per cent participation by the producing nations in existing concessions.

In 1966 such a request would have been spurned by the international oil companies. In early 1972 it was promptly agreed upon in principle.

Iraq's nationalization of the Iraq Petroleum Company follows a similar move in Algeria and the nationalization of the British Petroleum Company's properties in Libya.

The Iraqi seizure is seen as almost certain to harden the terms of the OPEC for 20 per cent participation.

In five years the oil industry has changed from a commanding ringmaster of a global enterprise to a sometimes unsure and often weak giant, looking for stability.

As Gulf War Intensifes, Oil Price Worries Grow

BY LEE A. DANIELS | JAN. 26, 1987

OIL SPECIALISTS IN the United States are deeply concerned that the escalation of the Iran-Iraq war could ultimately cause a significant shift in world oil supplies. Such a shift, by its very abruptness, could cause unsettling movements in price.

If there is a disruption in the supply of oil from the Persian Gulf, crude oil prices could be driven sharply higher at a time when the United States has greatly increased its oil imports, the specialists say.

On the other hand, if hostilities cool and exports from the region increase, prices could be forced down sharply, exacerbating the problems caused by the price crash of last year. Those included a sharp decline in United States oil production and severe financial difficulties for many oil companies and banks with large energy-related loans.

TURNING POINT SEEN IN WAR

As yet, the surge in fighting has not greatly affected activity on the world oil market, where prices have settled at about $18 a barrel. Daniel Yergin, president of Cambridge Energy Research Associates, a consulting firm in Cambridge, Mass., attributed this to the "jaded attitude" the oil community has developed toward what seemed to be an unending war.

However, Mr. Yergin added, the oil industry is now watching the battle for Basra, Iraq's second-largest city, "with increasing anxiety," because the seven-year-old war appears to be nearing a turning point.

A number of executives, analysts and consultants in the oil business said the lack of reliable information about the fighting makes it impossible to determine which country is gaining the upper hand.

Edward L. Morse, managing director of the Petroleum Finance Company, a Washington-based consulting firm, said, however: "The next two months are the most critical since the outbreak of the war. Iraq is beleaguered, and Iran is stretched extremely thin. This either will develop into a final offensive by Iran or set the stage for a negotiated settlement."

MANY POSSIBLE EFFECTS

The oil specialists said there are many ways the war's outcome could affect oil supplies, depending upon whether Iran or Iraq gains a conclusive victory, whether there is a negotiated settlement and whether the conflict continues at a low intensity.

For example, the chief executive of one large United States company, who asked to remain anonymous, said that an Iranian victory, or a negotiated settlement forced by Iran, could lead to higher oil prices.

He pointed out that Iran has long urged the Organization of Petroleum Exporting Countries to reduce its crude oil output substantially to raise prices. "They've consistently been much more hawkish on price than the OPEC moderates," the official said. "Twenty-five to twenty-eight dollars a barrel — that's their view of a right price for crude oil."

The more moderate OPEC states, such as Saudi Arabia, have indicated that for now their optimal crude oil price would be in the low $20's.

IRAN COULD WIELD CONTROL

The Persian Gulf states have recently become more accommodating toward Iran, while at the same time continuing their considerable support of Iraq. William B. Quandt, acting director of the Foreign Policy Program at the Brookings Institution in Washington, said that the Arab states have sought to play both sides against the middle during the conflict.

They fear that an unfettered Iran would foment fundamentalist uprisings within their borders. But they also dislike Iraq, which in the past has asserted that part of Kuwait is actually its territory.

Iran, with a population of 46 million, and Iraq, at 16 million, have substantially higher populations than Saudi Arabia, with an estimated 11.5 million, and most other neighbors.

Mr. Quandt said that Iranian gains in the war would induce "a very strong inclination to appease Iran" among the Persian Gulf countries.

In other words, three of OPEC's and the world's key oil producers — Saudi Arabia, Kuwait and the United Arab Emirates — would almost certainly acquiesce if Iran were to pointedly recommend that they reduce their crude oil output.

"Basically, they could dictate what the other countries' quotas would be," said Bryan Jacoboski, an oil analyst at Paine Webber Inc., "and that possibility is very worrisome to the oil industry."

Lawrence Goldstein, executive vice president of the Petroleum Industry Research Foundation, an industry group, said that if Iran were able to control Iraq's output, which has been exempted from the OPEC quota, American oil companies would have to consider accepting the long-term contracts for crude oil at fixed prices that some OPEC countries have been offering, rather than the month-by-month contracts they prefer.

On the other hand, a negotiated settlement of the war that left Iraqi production largely unaffected could contribute to a decline in prices, according to Mr. Morse, the oil consultant.

AIR ATTACKS CUT EXPORTS

The reason is that an end to the fighting would halt Iraqi air attacks on Iranian export facilities in the Persian Gulf. In the last eight months, those attacks have cut Iran's crude oil exports by as much as a third.

Mr. Morse said that if Iran were able to ship its crude oil freely, refiners would likely dump their sizable inventories, which would drive the price of oil down considerably.

Iran now produces about 1.8 million barrels a day, and exports 1.1 million barrels of that, according to the Petroleum Industry Research Foundation. Virtually all of Iran's exports are shipped through the Persian Gulf.

Iraq produces about 1.7 million barrels a day, and exports 1.4 million barrels, primarily through one pipeline to the Red Sea at Yanbu, Saudi Arabia, and through another to the Mediterranean at Dortyol, Turkey. The carrying capacity of both pipelines is being expanded, and many oil specialists say that Iraqi exports could grow to 2.5 million barrels a day by the end of the year.

However, Bryce Sachs, a principal in International Energy Consultants Ltd., of Morristown, N.J., said that, under yet another permutation of an end of the conflict, Iraq might not sharply increase its exports as the pipeline capacity becomes available.

Crude oil prices have risen as much as $3 a barrel since the latest OPEC accord took effect Jan. 1, in part because of the war's escalation and higher demand resulting from cold weather in Europe. However, James R. Schlesinger, the Energy Secretary under President Ford and now a consultant for Shearson Lehman Brothers, said that the fundamentals of the oil market — the volume of crude oil in inventories and the forthcoming drop-off in demand as winter ends — remain problematic.

Oil Exacts a Price From the Earth

OPINION | BY WILLIAM K. STEVENS | APRIL 2, 1989

A DECADE AGO, concern about pollution from oil spills reached a crescendo with what remain the two biggest disasters so far: the wreck of the tanker Amoco Cadiz off the coast of France in 1978, spilling 68 million gallons of crude oil along the Brittany shoreline, and the blowout of the Ixtoc I oil well in the Gulf of Mexico a year later, pouring 140 million gallons into the sea.

But in the 1980's, the issue faded from public consciousness partly because a more cautious oil industry, stung by costs and criticism, succeeded in significantly reducing the number of large spills. The spotlight shifted elsewhere as other environmental issues like toxic waste took center stage.

Now the grounding of the tanker Exxon Valdez in Alaska's Prince William Sound and the ecological and economic calamity caused by the escape of more than 10 million gallons of crude have brought the issue back to the forefront. But this time, the discussion has emerged amid increasing worry about the broader effects of fossil fuels on the environment.

So far attention has focused on the immediate circumstances of the worst disaster of its kind in American history: the ship captain's drinking, the control of the tanker by an unlicensed helmsman, the delay by Exxon in trying to contain the spill.

Some energy experts, looking beyond the immediate questions that are likely to be the subject of long and thorough investigation, say that the Exxon Valdez spill could be a warning of risks to come when, as is eventually bound to happen, world oil prices rise again and oil exploration expands into its last frontiers: the pristine, ecologically sensitive arctic and Antarctic regions where harsh conditions make it extremely difficult to deal with an oil spill, and where cold weather delays the natural decomposition of petroleum.

Environmentalists are not only seizing on the Exxon Valdez incident to bolster their case against oil drilling off the California and Florida coasts and in the Arctic National Wildlife Refuge in Alaska; they are also holding it up as one more example, along with urban air pollution and the greenhouse effect, of the cost of continuing dependence on fossil fuels.

Since its peak in 1979, the amount of oil lost worldwide at sea and on land through spillage, fire and sinkings has plummeted from 328 million gallons to between 24 million and 55 million a year, according to the Center for Short-Lived Phenomena in Cambridge, Mass., which keeps track of oil spills. There was one exceptional year, 1983, when well blowouts in the Iran-Iraq war and a rash of large tanker accidents swelled the total to 242 million gallons.

While the downward trend was being established, a study by the National Research Council found in 1985 that the most important source of oil pollution in the oceans was not well blowouts and tanker accidents but municipal and industrial runoff, the cleaning of ship bilges and other routine occurrences. The study also found that all the sources together posed less of an overall threat to the environment than many had thought.

Still, the study found, "petroleum can have a seriously adverse effect on local environments, persisting, in some cases unaltered, for decades."

Since large oil-spill disasters are "low-probability events," the Exxon Valdez disaster will most likely turn out to be an aberration, not the start of a new upward trend, said Richard S. Golob, director of the Cambridge center and an expert on oil spills. The United States, he said, has been particularly fortunate in having no major incidents since 1976, when the tanker Argo Merchant grounded off southeastern Massachusetts, spilling 7.6 million gallons of crude.

Still, these unlikely events are going to happen, he said, "no matter how well you plan in advance." And "in a massive spill situation, regardless of the degree of pre-planning, all hell breaks loose," he said.

"The reason is that it takes place so infrequently, and the resources are never available in a single location to deal effectively with it," he said.

A LOSS OF EXPERTISE

One problem, in Mr. Golob's view, is that the decline in big accidents in the 1980's caused the Government to shift its attention toward hazardous waste and toxic chemicals. Funds for oil-spill response and research "have decreased dramatically," he said, and the oil industry, in a wave of economy moves in the 1980's, has let many of its most experienced experts on spills retire early.

Throughout the 1980's, some environmentalists have been insisting that although oil spill disasters have declined, smaller spills are taking place all the time, with adverse effects on ecosystems and wildlife. It is a "chronic problem," said Lisa Speer, a senior scientist at the Natural Resources Defense Council, an environmental group based in New York. "The only way to protect areas that are economically and ecologically valuable is to keep oil out," she said.

The Exxon Valdez incident is sure to provoke new argument about opening up more coastal areas, along with the Alaskan wildlife refuge, to oil exploration. Proponents of increased exploration say that failure to exploit those reserves will once again lay the United States open to the mercy of foreign producers. In 10 or 15 years, "demand for oil will be high enough so that they can dictate the price again," said Charles J. DiBona, president of the American Petroleum Institute, an industry trade group. "To choose not to develop the Alaskan refuge in the face of falling domestic production would be a big economic and political and security decision for this country," he said. A Senate committee has approved legislation opening the refuge to exploration, and President Bush favors it.

But the big energy issue of the 1990's is not going to be the depletion of oil resources, said Daniel Yergin, president of Cambridge Energy Research Associates. "The environment is going to be the big theme," he said. Most new oil will be found "in very tough and treacherous conditions" in the far nothern and far southern latitudes, he said, where cold, icebergs and heavy seas increase the risk of oil spills and pollution.

Although the world seems to have cast its lot with oil for the foreseeable future, some environmentalists are finding in the Exxon Valdez incident new justification for switching from fossil fuels to renewable energy sources like solar power. The tragedy in Alaska has its roots in the dependence on fossil fuels, said Joseph Goffman, a senior attorney for the Environmental Defense Fund, which is based in New York. But he said that oil spills, air pollution, acid rain and global warming caused by the greenhouse effect all come back to the same underlying problem. The use of fossil fuels, he said, "is the central knot that's got to be untied."

WILLIAM K. STEVENS is a science reporter for The New York Times.

Iraq Deploys Troops Near Kuwait Border Amid Dispute on Oil

SPECIAL TO THE NEW YORK TIMES | JULY 24, 1990

WASHINGTON, JULY 23 — American military officials are closely watching a new deployment of thousands of troops by Iraq along its border with Kuwait, where recent political tensions appeared to be escalating into armed posturing by the two Persian Gulf nations, Pentagon officials said tonight.

A senior Pentagon official said tonight that he viewed the movement of troops by Iraq as posturing. He said he had no reason to expect the situation to erupt into fighting, but that the Pentagon is watching it closely.

The Washington Post reported that a group of Western military attaches traveling to Baghdad during the weekend had seen thousands of Iraqi vehicles moving south toward Kuwait, including tanks, armored personnel carriers and missile launchers. The Post said that military attaches believed Iraq was massing 30,000 troops in the area.

The Post said that American forces in the region had been told to stand ready in case a response was needed, but Navy officials last night did not comment on that aspect of the report.

The United States has several ships in the Persian Gulf, where Kuwaiti tankers flying the American flag were provided escorts during the Iran-Iraq war to protect them against Iranian attack.

Iraq and Kuwait have been engaged in an increasingly virulent dispute over oil production quotas in recent days, as members of the Oil Producing and Exporting Countries prepare for a major meeting to try to shore up prices.

Although Kuwait supported Iraq financially in its long war with Iran, since the war ended long-standing frictions between Kuwait and Iraq have resurfaced.

Last week Iraq accused Kuwait of stealing oil by drilling on Iraqi territory, and of deploying troops on Iraqi territory. At the same time, Iraq complained that Kuwait and the United Arab Emirates, had been depressing oil prices by exceeding their OPEC production quotas.

A War for Oil?

OPINION | BY THOMAS L. FRIEDMAN | JAN. 5, 2003

OUR FAMILY SPENT winter vacation in Colorado, and one day I saw the most unusual site: two women marching around the Aspen Mountain ski lift, waving signs protesting against war in Iraq. One sign said: "Just War or Just Oil?" As I watched this two-woman demonstration, I couldn't help notice the auto traffic whizzing by them: one gas-guzzling S.U.V. or Jeep after another, with even a Humvee or two tossed in for good measure. The whole scene made me wonder whether those two women weren't — indeed — asking the right question: Is the war that the Bush team is preparing to launch in Iraq really a war for oil?

My short answer is yes. Any war we launch in Iraq will certainly be — in part — about oil. To deny that is laughable. But whether it is seen to be only about oil will depend on how we behave before an invasion and what we try to build once we're there.

I say this possible Iraq war is partly about oil because it is impossible to explain the Bush team's behavior otherwise. Why are they going after Saddam Hussein with the 82nd Airborne and North Korea with diplomatic kid gloves — when North Korea already has nuclear weapons, the missiles to deliver them, a record of selling dangerous weapons to anyone with cash, 100,000 U.S. troops in its missile range and a leader who is even more cruel to his own people than Saddam?

One reason, of course, is that it is easier to go after Saddam. But the other reason is oil — even if the president doesn't want to admit it. (Mr. Bush's recent attempt to hype the Iraqi threat by saying that an Iraqi attack on America — which is most unlikely — "would cripple our economy" was embarrassing. It made the president look as if he was groping for an excuse to go to war, absent a smoking gun.)

Let's cut the nonsense. The primary reason the Bush team is more focused on Saddam is because if he were to acquire weapons of mass destruction, it might give him the leverage he has long sought — not to attack us, but to extend his influence over the world's largest source of oil, the Persian Gulf.

But wait a minute. There is nothing illegitimate or immoral about the U.S. being concerned that an evil, megalomaniacal dictator might acquire excessive influence over the natural resource that powers the world's industrial base.

"Would those women protesting in Aspen prefer that Saddam Hussein control the oil instead — is that morally better?" asks Michael Mandelbaum, the Johns Hopkins foreign policy expert and author of "The Ideas That Conquered the World." "Up to now, Saddam has used his oil wealth not to benefit his people, but to wage war against all his neighbors, build lavish palaces and acquire weapons of mass destruction."

This is a good point, but the Bush team would have a stronger case for fighting a war partly for oil if it made clear by its behavior that it was acting for the benefit of the planet, not simply to fuel American excesses.

I have no problem with a war for oil — if we accompany it with a real program for energy conservation. But when we tell the world that we couldn't care less about climate change, that we feel entitled to drive whatever big cars we feel like, that we feel entitled to consume however much oil we like, the message we send is that a war for oil in the gulf is not a war to protect the world's right to economic survival — but our right to indulge. Now that will be seen as immoral.

And should we end up occupying Iraq, and the first thing we do is hand out drilling concessions to U.S. oil companies alone, that perception would only be intensified.

And that leads to my second point. If we occupy Iraq and simply install a more pro-U.S. autocrat to run the Iraqi gas station (as we have in other Arab oil states), then this war partly for oil would also be immoral.

If, on the other hand, the Bush team, and the American people, prove willing to stay in Iraq and pay the full price, in money and manpower, needed to help Iraqis build a more progressive, democratizing Arab state — one that would use its oil income for the benefit of all its people and serve as a model for its neighbors — then a war partly over oil would be quite legitimate. It would be a critical step toward building a better Middle East.

So, I have no problem with a war for oil — provided that it is to fuel the first progressive Arab regime, and not just our S.U.V.'s, and provided we behave in a way that makes clear to the world we are protecting everyone's access to oil at reasonable prices — not simply our right to binge on it.

THOMAS L. FRIEDMAN is an Op-Ed columnist for The New York Times.

Shale Boom in Texas Could Increase U.S. Oil Output

BY CLIFFORD KRAUSS | MAY 27, 2011

CATARINA, TEX. — Until last year, the 17-mile stretch of road between this forsaken South Texas village and the county seat of Carrizo Springs was a patchwork of derelict gasoline stations and rusting warehouses.

Now the region is in the hottest new oil play in the country, with giant oil terminals and sprawling RV parks replacing fields of mesquite. More than a dozen companies plan to drill up to 3,000 wells around here in the next 12 months.

The Texas field, known as the Eagle Ford, is just one of about 20 new onshore oil fields that advocates say could collectively increase the nation's oil output by 25 percent within a decade — without the dangers of drilling in the deep waters of the Gulf of Mexico or the delicate coastal areas off Alaska.

There is only one catch: the oil from the Eagle Ford and similar fields of tightly packed rock can be extracted only by using hydraulic fracturing, a method that uses a high-pressure mix of water, sand and hazardous chemicals to blast through the rocks to release the oil inside.

The technique, also called fracking, has been widely used in the last decade to unlock vast new fields of natural gas, but drillers only recently figured out how to release large quantities of oil, which flows less easily through rock than gas. As evidence mounts that fracking poses risks to water supplies, the federal government and regulators in various states are considering tighter regulations on it.

The oil industry says any environmental concerns are far outweighed by the economic benefits of pumping previously inaccessible oil from fields that could collectively hold two or three times as much oil as Prudhoe Bay, the Alaskan field that was the last great onshore

MICHAEL STRAVATO FOR THE NEW YORK TIMES

An RV park has sprung up near a road in Carrizo Springs, Tex., to house an influx of oil field workers because of a lack of housing and hotels in the area.

discovery. The companies estimate that the boom will create more than two million new jobs, directly or indirectly, and bring tens of billions of dollars to the states where the fields are located, which include traditional oil sites like Texas and Oklahoma, industrial stalwarts like Ohio and Michigan and even farm states like Kansas.

"It's the one thing we have seen in our adult lives that could take us away from imported oil," said Aubrey McClendon, chief executive of Chesapeake Energy, one of the most aggressive drillers. "What if we have found three of the world's biggest oil fields in the last three years right here in the U.S.? How transformative could that be for the U.S. economy?"

The oil rush is already transforming this impoverished area of Texas near the Mexican border, doubling real estate values in the last year and filling restaurants and hotels.

"That's oil money," said Bert Bell, a truck company manager, pointing to the new pickup truck he bought for his wife after making $525,000 leasing mineral rights around his family's mobile home. "Oil money just makes life easier."

Based on the industry's plans, shale and other "tight rock" fields that now produce about half a million barrels of oil a day will produce up to three million barrels daily by 2020, according to IHS CERA, an energy research firm. Oil companies are investing an estimated $25 billion this year to drill 5,000 new oil wells in tight rock fields, according to Raoul LeBlanc, a senior director at PFC Energy, a consulting firm.

"This is very big and it's coming on very fast," said Daniel Yergin, the chairman of IHS CERA. "This is like adding another Venezuela or Kuwait by 2020, except these tight oil fields are in the United States."

In the most developed shale field, the Bakken field in North Dakota, production has leaped to 400,000 barrels a day today from a trickle four years ago. Experts say it could produce as much as a million barrels a day by the end of the decade.

The Eagle Ford, where the first well was drilled only three years ago, is already producing more than 100,000 barrels a day and could reach 420,000 by 2015, almost as much as Ecuador, according to Bentek Energy, a consultancy.

The shale oil boom comes as production from Prudhoe Bay is declining and drilling in the Gulf of Mexico is being more closely scrutinized after last year's Deepwater Horizon disaster.

What makes the new fields more remarkable is that they were thought to be virtually valueless only five years ago. "Everyone said the oil molecules are too large to flow in commercial quantities through these low-quality rocks," said Mark G. Papa, chief executive of EOG Resources.

EOG began quietly buying the rights to thousands of acres in the Bakken and Eagle Ford after an EOG engineer concluded that the techniques used to extract natural gas from shale — fracking, combined with drilling horizontally through layers of rocks — could be used for

MICHAEL STRAVATO FOR THE NEW YORK TIMES

A Chesapeake Energy drilling site near Big Wells, Tex.

oil. Chesapeake and a few other independents quickly followed. Now the biggest multinational oil companies, as well as Chinese and Norwegian firms, are investing billions of dollars in the fields.

The new drilling makes economic sense as long as oil prices remain above $60 a barrel, according to oil companies. At current oil prices of about $100 a barrel, shale wells can typically turn a profit within eight months — three times faster than many traditional wells.

But water remains a key issue. In addition to possible contamination of surface and underground water from fracking fluids, the sheer volume of water required poses challenges, especially in South Texas, which faces a severe drought and rapidly diminishing water levels in the local aquifer.

At the rate wells are being drilled, "there's definitely going to be a problem," said Bay Laxson, a local water official.

Dave Thompson, regional production superintendent for the oil company SM Energy said the industry knew that water issues were "an Achilles heel." He said his company was building a system to reuse water in the field.

But unlike Pennsylvania and New York, where fracking for natural gas has produced organized opposition, the oil industry has been mostly welcomed in western and southern states.

Thanks to the drilling boom, the recession bypassed North Dakota entirely. Here in Dimmit County, Tex., the unemployment rate has fallen in half, and sales tax receipts are up 70 percent so far this year, allowing the county to hire more police officers and buy sanitation and road repair equipment.

"In my lifetime, this is the biggest thing I've ever seen," said Jose Gonzalez, 78, a retired teacher and son of migrant farm workers, who leased mineral rights to Chesapeake for $27,000 and sold another plot for $100,000 to a company building an RV park for oil workers. "You can see I'm happy."

Out of Africa (and Elsewhere): More Fossil Fuels

BY MARK SCOTT | APRIL 10, 2012

THE WORLD'S LARGEST energy companies have big plans for Mozambique.

Until recently, the East African country was better known for its long civil war, and had few energy resources compared with regional heavy-hitters like Nigeria and Angola.

But in the last 10 years, companies like Exxon Mobil, the BG Group of Britain and Eni of Italy have used the latest technologies, including advances in deep-sea drilling, to find new natural gas resources that are turning Mozambique into the center of an energy boom.

Up and down the country's shoreline, Western energy companies, as well as a number of Asian competitors, are drilling wells thousands of feet below the Indian Ocean in hopes of striking it rich. The rewards could be huge. Mozambique may have more deposits of natural gas — used in everything from manufacturing to electricity generation — than the European energy giant Norway.

The East African country is not alone in its newfound energy wealth. Countries like Tanzania and Kenya also are attracting billions of dollars in investment from the world's largest energy companies as they search for new oil and gas reserves.

"Africa will be the backbone of our production and growth in the next 10 years," Paolo Scaroni, chief executive of Italian energy giant Eni, told investors last month in London.

In total, the Italian company expects to spend $50 billion to develop natural gas projects off the coast of Mozambique. While production may not start until the end of the decade, the energy firm has designated the new reserves for customers in fast-growing Asian markets like India and China.

Other companies, including Anadarko Petroleum of Texas, also have multibillion-dollar plans for such new African oil and gas finds. Most, too, expect to sell the energy to emerging economies hungry to drive domestic growth.

The quickening pace of exploration in East Africa is part of a wider shake-up in the global energy industry as it scrambles to adapt to a series of major changes. Those range from the nuclear disaster in Japan last year, to slashed subsidies for alternative energy amid Europe's economic crisis, to a boom in unconventional fossil fuels like shale gas that has spread across continents.

The changes have been particularly drastic in fast-growing China, now the world's largest energy user and emitter of carbon dioxide. Since opening its economy over three decades ago, the Asian giant has become an insatiable consumer of natural resources. The country still relies predominantly on dirty coal for its electricity, but has fast-tracked oil production, as well as newer technologies like shale gas, and hydroelectric and wind power, to maintain its high levels of domestic growth.

With demand from emerging economies continuing apace, the quest for new fossil fuels is opening up unexplored territories for production. That may help to offset the effect of rising oil prices, which have reached almost record highs.

"The demand from billions of people worldwide to consume energy isn't slowing down," said Adi Karev, the global head of the oil and gas practice at the consultancy Deloitte in Hong Kong. "Companies' ability to find new energy reserves, especially in remote locations, is altering the global market."

The opportunities are welcome in more ways than one. The new discoveries, including the so-called tar sands of Canada, are allowing Western companies like Royal Dutch Shell and BP to diversify and safeguard future production. State-owned firms like Sinopec of China and Gazprom of Russia have slowly taken over production of their domestic reserves, leaving them in control of roughly 85 percent of the world's oil resources, according to the Energy Information Administration.

The discoveries also are helping countries from the United States to Romania to decrease their dependence on foreign energy imports as well as generate tax revenue and employment.

Poland presents a case in point. Since 2009, Chevron and other Western energy giants have been exploring there for shale gas, using many of the techniques pioneered in the United States. The new energy resources could have a major effect on Poland, which currently imports more than 80 percent of its natural gas from Russia, its once dominant neighbor. The potential reserves may provide Poland with enough gas for more than 50 years, according to the country's national geological institute.

"There's a real desire in Poland to build their own natural gas supplies," said Ian MacDonald, Chevron's general manager for business development and transportation. "They recognize that there's a national interest."

So far, the American energy company has been drilling test wells to figure out how much shale gas can be extracted. Chevron has permits to explore more than one million acres in the southeast of Poland. It expects to have a clear picture of the potential size of the region's energy reserves by the end of next year.

All may not go smoothly. Europe's shale gas industry is not as developed as that of the United States, so finding the right drilling equipment and qualified work force could limit production.

Public perception may prove a problem, too. This year, Bulgaria canceled drilling permits for Chevron, and banned the controversial drilling technology known as hydraulic fracturing, or fracking, which some environmental advocates have linked to the contamination of drinking water. France also prohibited the technique last year.

"We're working with governments and communities to explain what we're doing," Mr. MacDonald said. "Shale gas has the potential to be an enormous economic benefit."

The emerging fossil fuel renaissance, however, has not been good news for every energy company. In the alternative sector, wind farms and solar panels now find it that much harder to compete against fossil fuels, given the new oil and gas discoveries. Analysts say electricity from wind farms located off the coasts of Britain and Germany, for example, may cost six times as much compared with power plants that burn coal or natural gas.

Cutbacks in government subsidies for renewable energy, particularly in European countries struggling from the Continent's sovereign debt crisis, also are taking a toll. Western companies, including Vestas of Denmark and Q.Cells of Germany, already face tough competition from Asian rivals. Now, cash-poor countries are paring back price guarantees and canceling tax credits for green energy projects.

"The financial crisis has turned off the government tap for renewables investment," said Ronan O'Regan, director of renewables and clean technology at PricewaterhouseCoopers in London.

The changing economics are forcing green energy companies to adapt. Faced with falling global prices for wind turbines and solar panels, analysts expect the industry's largest manufacturers to buy, or merge with, rivals, as they look to strengthen their market positions. Deals are already taking place. Last year, takeovers in the world's renewables industry totaled $53.5 billion, a 40 percent increase over 2010, according to PricewaterhouseCoopers.

Others are looking for cash-rich investors. In a bizarre twist, traditional oil and gas companies may come to the rescue of many green energy projects. With decades of experience developing resources out at sea, traditional energy companies are focusing their attention on multibillion-dollar plans to build wind farms off the coast of Europe and North America. Over the last 18 months, for example, the Spanish oil company Repsol and its Norwegian rival Statoil have announced investments in offshore wind projects across Northern Europe.

Interest in nuclear power also has waned after last year's disaster involving the Fukushima Daiichi nuclear power plant in Japan. Before the accident, there were 440 reactors in operation worldwide, with a further 558 plants either under construction or on the drawing board, according to the consultant Capgemini.

Now Japan has shut almost all of its nuclear reactors, and countries like Germany and Italy have either announced plans to close their remaining plants or canceled efforts to build new facilities. Asian countries are building the largest number of new nuclear power plants, though analysts say the pace of construction has slowed by almost a quarter in the last 12 months.

"The development of new plants has slowed down, but India and China remain committed to building new nuclear capacity," said Colette Lewiner, Capgemini's global head of utilities, energy and chemicals in Paris.

With the outlook dimming for low-carbon energy sources like nuclear power and renewables, there are growing concerns that efforts to curb global greenhouse gas emissions will fail as countries look to exploit new sources of fossil fuels.

Levels of carbon dioxide, for example, rose 5.9 percent in 2010, the latest figures available, according to the Global Carbon Project, an international collaboration of scientists that tracks the numbers. The increase came despite a slowdown in global manufacturing, as many of the world's largest economies struggled because of the financial crisis.

With many countries expected to return to growth, the use of fossil fuels — and the resulting emissions — are expected to rise.

"Finding new deposits doesn't change the climate constraints facing the world," said Dan Lashof, director of the climate center at the Natural Resources Defense Council in Washington. "We can't continue to indefinitely burn fossil fuels."

Lessons From the Exxon Valdez Oil Spill

BY HENRY FOUNTAIN | DEC. 9, 2013

On a cold March night in 1989, the tanker Exxon Valdez ran aground off the coast of Alaska, spilling 11 million gallons of crude oil into the waters of Prince William Sound and creating one of the worst oil spills in American history. This week's Retro Report examines how that spill happened and follows its impact over the past twenty-five years. Here, a Times reporter who covered the BP oil disaster of 2010 writes about how containment and cleanup evolved.

AS OIL DISASTERS GO, the 1989 Exxon Valdez grounding and the 2010 Deepwater Horizon blowout were about as different as two spills could be.

One wasn't even technically a spill. When the Deepwater Horizon exploded and sank in the Gulf of Mexico, it uncorked a gusher, a mile down at the seabed. This subsea torrent of oil turned out to be far greater than the amount of crude that leaked from the damaged Exxon Valdez onto the surface of Prince William Sound — about 200 million gallons compared with 11 million — and it posed a different set of problems for BP and government officials.

In cleaning up an oil spill, a main goal is to separate the oil from the water — like skimming the fat off a bowl of gravy. In the gulf disaster, it didn't help that cleanup technologies like booms and skimmers had changed little over two decades. But the fact that the oil spewed into the deep gulf waters and spread out over a wide area before it reached the surface made containing and collecting the oil even harder.

As a result, the government allowed BP to try something new: injecting chemical dispersants into the plume of oil at the seabed. Ordinarily, dispersants help break surface oil into tiny droplets that sink into the water column, where they can be degraded by bacteria. That was the goal in Prince William Sound. In the gulf, the hope was that the chemicals would keep the oil from reaching the surface.

It is unclear how effective the technique was, and subsequent studies have suggested that the large amount of dispersants — close to two million gallons in all, far more than in any other spill — might have left their own detrimental environmental effects.

For BP, the cleanup was only half the battle. The Exxon Valdez carried a huge but finite amount of oil, while the gulf well could have continued gushing for months or years if it wasn't stopped. That is where BP, the rest of the industry and the government were really unprepared. They had no experience in trying to control a deepwater blowout. The well was only 5,000 feet away, but because no human could reach it, it might as well have been on Mars.

Technology had failed BP's engineers. The subsea blowout preventer — the enormous array of pipes and valves that sat atop the well at the seabed — had not done its job during the initial emergency, and in the first few days of the disaster all the remotely operated submersibles in the world could not get it to shut the gusher down.

That left the engineers and well-control specialists to attempt jury-rigged solutions. For months none of these efforts — with nicknames like "junk shot," "top kill" and "top hat" — worked. What eventually did tame the well was a large "capping stack" that fit snugly atop the blowout preventer. To the engineers' credit, they had thought of this early on. When I met with some of them at BP in Houston two weeks into the disaster, the idea of such a device was mentioned, but it took two months to design and build it.

After that experience, most of the major companies that drill in the gulf, including BP, formed an independent company to come up with equipment and procedures for dealing with future spills. The company, Marine Well Containment, has built an all-purpose capping stack and other equipment, and more work is planned. The idea is to have the equipment ready, along with people trained to use it, should another deep-sea blowout occur.

Then again, the next disaster may be completely different, just as the Deepwater Horizon disaster was from the Exxon Valdez.

BP May Be Fined Up to $18 Billion for Spill in Gulf

BY CAMPBELL ROBERTSON AND CLIFFORD KRAUSS | SEPT. 4, 2014

NEW ORLEANS — In the four years since the blowout on the Deepwater Horizon oil rig killed 11 workers and sent millions of barrels of oil gushing into the Gulf of Mexico, BP has spent more than $28 billion on damage claims and cleanup costs, pleaded guilty to criminal charges and emerged a shrunken giant.

But through it all, the company has maintained that it was not chiefly responsible for the accident, and that its contractors in the operation, Halliburton and Transocean, should shoulder as much, if not more, of the blame.

On Thursday, a federal judge here for the first time bluntly rejected those arguments, finding that BP was indeed the primary culprit and that only it had acted with "conscious disregard of known risks." He added that BP's "conduct was reckless."

By finding that BP was, in legal parlance, grossly negligent in the disaster, and not merely negligent, United States District Court Judge Carl J. Barbier opened the possibility of $18 billion in new civil penalties for BP, nearly quadruple the maximum Clean Water Act penalty for simple negligence and far more than the $3.5 billion the company has set aside.

The ruling stands as a milestone in environmental law given that this was the biggest offshore oil spill in American history, legal experts said, and serves as a warning for the oil companies that continue to drill in the deep waters of the Gulf of Mexico, where high pressures and temperatures in the wells test the most modern drilling technologies.

"We are pleased," United States Attorney General Eric H. Holder Jr. said of the ruling. "The court's finding will ensure that the company is held fully accountable for its recklessness."

The decision also casts a cloud over BP's future. Its reputation has already been sullied and important holdings in Russia are at risk because of tensions in Ukraine. In addition to the $28 billion in claim payments and cleanup costs it has paid, BP has been forced to divest itself of more than 10 percent of its oil and gas reserves, along with valuable pipelines and refining facilities to pay claims and increase its profitability. BP shares fell by nearly 6 percent Thursday, closing at $44.89.

In a statement, BP said it "strongly disagrees with the decision" and would immediately appeal to the United States Court of Appeals for the Fifth Circuit. BP added that the ruling was "not supported by the evidence at trial," and that "the law is clear that proving gross negligence is a very high bar that was not met in this case."

In a toughly worded 153-page decision, Judge Barbier reconstructed the timeline from the risky decision to drill more deeply before stopping to the hellish final minutes of hissing gas and raining mud, concluding with the deadly fireball that erupted on the night of April 20, 2010.

The hasty effort to temporarily shut down a drilling operation that was over budget and behind schedule led to what Judge Barbier called "a chain of failures" culminating in the explosion and spill.

Vital seals and stoppers were left leaky along the casing of the well, the judge found, while BP then skimped on tests that might have shown the problems caused by the shoddy work. When tests were run, the results were interpreted with optimism at best and dishonesty at worst, and several critical decisions made by BP were found by Judge Barbier to have been "primarily driven by a desire to save time and money, rather than ensuring that the well was secure."

In a central episode, Judge Barbier highlighted a phone call between a senior BP employee on the rig and an engineer in Houston that took place roughly 40 minutes before the explosion. In the call, the two men discussed the results of a pressure test that should have prompted quick action to prevent an impending blowout. BP did not mention this call in its own investigative report, an omission Judge Barbier found suspicious.

While acknowledging responsibility for the accident, BP had long argued that the blame should be fully shared with Transocean, the owner of the Deepwater Horizon oil rig, and Halliburton, a contractor that oversaw a critical step in closing up the well.

While Judge Barbier did find the other companies had acted with negligence, he concluded that only BP, which leased the well and was in charge of the operation, was grossly negligent. He apportioned 67 percent of the blame for the spill to BP, 30 percent to Transocean and 3 percent to Halliburton.

"Transocean's failures," the judge wrote at one point, "largely concern its inability (due in part to further failures by BP) to stop the catastrophe BP set in motion."

BP has already pleaded guilty to manslaughter and other charges and agreed to pay $4 billion in federal criminal penalties. But the company's ultimate civil liability is far from determined.

In 2012, BP reached a settlement with many of the individual and business plaintiffs but has battled in court over interpretations of that settlement ever since. Last month the company requested that the United States Supreme Court support its reading of the settlement after a federal appeals court rejected that argument in May.

The leaders of a group of lawyers representing the damage claimants, James P. Roy and Stephen J. Herman, reacted to Thursday's ruling in a statement, saying, "The court has now laid bare the full extent of the level of BP's misconduct."

Officials from states along the gulf welcomed Thursday's decision as ammunition for their own separate damage lawsuits.

"Armed with this finding," Alabama's attorney general, Luther Strange, said in a statement, "Alabama is preparing to prosecute its case for compensatory and punitive damages against BP."

The ruling only pertains to the first phase of a federal civil trial, concerning the responsibility of the blowout itself. Judge Barbier still must rule on how much oil was spilled in the accident, the subject of a trial that took place in the fall of last year. A third phase, scheduled to start in January, will lead to a final determination of penalties under the Clean Water Act.

This week Halliburton reached a $1.1 billion settlement with individual and business plaintiffs. Last year, Transocean agreed to pay $1.4 billion to settle federal criminal and civil charges, which is likely to cover most of its liability.

Legal scholars said BP faced an uphill struggle in the appeals process.

David M. Uhlmann, a law professor at the University of Michigan, who headed the environmental crimes section of the Justice Department from 2000 to 2007, highlighted the judge's decision that "the government did not need to show BP was aware of the risks associated with its conduct" to be found grossly negligent.

But the judge went on to say, Mr. Uhlmann said, that "even if they had to show awareness of risk, the government had satisfied that burden."

CAMPBELL ROBERTSON reported from New Orleans and **CLIFFORD KRAUSS** from New York. John Schwartz contributed reporting from New Orleans.

Oil Firms Learn to Move an Ancient Product With New-Age Tech

BY STANLEY REED | OCT. 14, 2017

SUNBURY-ON-THAMES, ENGLAND — BP's troubleshooters here received a call for help from colleagues in Azerbaijan. Sand was invading oil wells from the rocks outside. To avoid damage, the operators were choking the wells back, reducing revenues.

Two tech-savvy specialists, Prad Thiruvenkatanathan, a research scientist, and Tommy Langnes, a sand expert, came up with a novel fix. They used fiber-optic cable to gather the sounds coming from the wells deep in the earth. Inspired by apps like Shazam that recognize the voices of pop stars, they figured how to distinguish the sonic signature of sand from other sounds, like flowing oil. They also installed computers on the production platforms to sift staggering volumes of data coming from the wells down to manageable levels.

Using these tools, BP can identify where sand is coming in and patch the breaches instead of choking down the whole well. The flows from one well have already increased by nearly 50 percent, potentially a huge gain if the technology is rolled out through BP's global network, where sand is a common problem. They are already using a similar tool to detect leaks and other potential hazards.

"It is just like your iPhone," Mr. Langnes said. "We have built the phone. We have a couple of apps installed. Now the R&D team is working on new apps to install on the digital platform."

The oil industry has long been of two minds when it comes to high technology. Oil companies like BP and Italy's Eni use powerful supercomputers to crunch data from sound waves into images of petroleum deposits in the ground. Yet the industry has been resistant to change in other areas, like the process of producing oil.

On weather-battered offshore platforms in Britain's North Sea, for instance, technicians still walk around with "big pieces of paper in the rain, wind," said Claire Day, a BP operations engineer. "It is not an ideal way to work."

Change, though, is coming as companies like BP and Statoil, the Norwegian oil company, embrace technology to help cut costs. Anders Brun, a consultant in the oil and gas practice at McKinsey & Company, says analyzing huge amount of data to optimize processes like oil production and automate activities like drilling is the logical next step.

Before oil prices plunged in 2014, Mr. Brun said, gaining access to natural resources rather than cost-cutting was the priority. Now the heads of the big oil companies, inspired by what they see in areas like banking, retailing and mining, want to do the same. McKinsey estimates that through activities like using big data to analyze the performance of various production platforms, oil companies can improve their profits by up to $11 per barrel, or $300 billion a year by 2025.

"The potential is quite staggering," he said.

Companies are forging ahead in some key areas. BP, for instance, is experimenting with automating drilling on natural gas wells in a new field in Oman. BP would like the driller's role to be more like that of an airplane pilot, who oversees the computers actually fine-tuning the plane.

Leigh-Ann Russell, a drilling executive, said that automation would make operations safer by taking people off installations and out of harm's way. By reducing the chances of human error that she said was responsible for most safety incidents, automating drilling rigs would also improve business performance, because a lot of waste "is often caused by human error as well."

Oil companies are also very gingerly experimenting with technology that can help remove people from offshore platforms, which produce much of the world's oil. Any job that can be moved to land represents a big saving because offshore workers are highly paid and need to be housed, fed and rotated every few weeks by helicopter.

When BP recently moved a drilling rig 350 miles across the North Sea, the three-person team responsible for positioning the vessel, remained on land. They worked from the company's hub in Aberdeen, Scotland, through a remote positioning and monitoring system. BP estimates that keeping teams "on the beach" will save $20,000 on each of these moves.

The employees that remain on the rigs may receive cellphones and computer tablets insulated to avoid sparks that could set off explosions. The intention is for them to use these devices to click through tasks like maintenance checks, enter data and hear back quickly if something is wrong.

"Your training burden is massively reduced as well," said Ms. Day. "No one has taught any of us how to use Facebook or WhatsApp. You just pick them up."

Still, some observers think it will not be easy to make radical changes, especially on offshore platforms, where workers may think they have enough to do without learning new tricks.

Andrew Tidey, global head of performance improvement at energy consultants Wood Mackenzie, said that people in control rooms might already have more information than they could manage.

"Is the real issue information or is it human behavior?" he asked. "We will see how that plays out."

CHAPTER 3

Natural Gas and a New Age of Fossil Fuels

Natural gas is a fossil fuel often found near oil or coal deposits. Its use had been limited until the 20th century, when technologies for isolating and delivering the gas — mostly methane — from oil wells or underground reservoirs improved. Natural gas has a large market in the United States, where people use it for heating and cooking, and where it can be used to produce plastics or other chemical products. Often marketed as a "clean" fuel, at least in comparison to oil and coal, natural gas extraction and consumption come with their own environmental risks that have to be weighed against the potential economic benefits.

Study Says Natural Gas Use Likely to Double

BY MATTHEW L. WALD | JUNE 25, 2010

WASHINGTON — Natural gas will provide an increasing share of America's energy needs over the next several decades, doubling its share of the energy market to 40 percent, from 20 percent, according to a report to be released Friday by the Massachusetts Institute of Technology.

The increase, the report concluded, will come largely at the expense of coal and will be driven both by abundant supplies of natural gas —

made more available by shale drilling — and by measures to restrict the carbon dioxide emissions that are linked to climate change.

In the long term, however, the future may be dimmer for natural gas if stricter regulations are put in place to cut greenhouse gas emissions by 80 percent below 1990 levels by 2050 — a goal set by President Obama. Although lower in carbon than coal, natural gas is still too carbon-intensive to be used under such a target absent some method of carbon capture, the authors of the report concluded.

The report, one of a series on energy resources, is the result of a two-year effort by 14 prominent energy experts, led by Ernest J. Moniz, an M.I.T. professor who is a former under secretary of energy. Previous reports focused on nuclear power and coal. The report was financed in part by the American Clean Skies Foundation, which represents the interests of the natural gas industry.

In the report, the authors point out that there is a mismatch between current energy practice in the United States and the nation's energy goals. As zero-carbon wind is added to the national electric system, the report said, it is being used to reduce consumption of natural gas, which is relatively benign in carbon impact, rather than coal, which has twice as much carbon dioxide per kilowatt-hour. The reason is that gas is more expensive than coal.

Gas will eventually replace some of the coal used to make electricity, the study predicts, and gas will be the benchmark against which other carbon-saving technologies like wind or nuclear will be measured. But those other technologies will eventually be needed.

Some companies that make equipment for coal- and gas-fired generating stations say that the switch to gas from coal has already begun. One reason is that switching to gas will make it easier to meet air quality standards for conventional pollutants, like smog and mercury.

The study noted that the only natural gas car sold by a major car company in the United States, the Honda GX, costs an extra $5,500, while the VW Passat TSI Eco-fuel, sold only in Europe, costs only $3,700 extra. Converting a gasoline vehicle to natural gas is also much more expensive here than in Europe, the report said, and it suggests that the reasons be examined.

High-mileage fleet vehicles, like taxis, could be economically converted to natural gas, the study said. But the recent history of natural gas vehicles in the United States suggests that buses and small delivery vehicles are more likely candidates for conversion than the great mass of privately owned vehicles.

Natural gas vehicles emit about three-quarters as much carbon dioxide per mile as gasoline-powered ones. The switch would not have a large impact on carbon — only about a ton per vehicle per year for a typical American car, according to the report.

"There is no longer any doubt that we have the capacity to repower our electricity sector and move away from dirtier fuels," said Gregory C. Staple, the chief executive of the American Clean Skies Foundation, in a statement.

T. Boone Pickens, the Texas oilman, said that the study paid too much attention to the electricity sector and not enough to using natural gas as a substitute for gasoline and diesel in transportation.

"You've got plenty of gas to do both," he said.

Natural gas has an erratic price history, which has made some American electric utilities nervous about overreliance. But "abundant global natural gas resources imply greatly expanded natural gas use," the study concluded.

Globally, the average projection of the amount of recoverable gas represents about a century and a half's supply at current rates of consumption, the report noted. In the United States, the amount of recoverable gas is equal to 92 times the consumption last year, the study said.

Especially in the United States, one reason for new optimism about supplies is the success that drillers have had exploring shale formations for natural gas. Shale drilling requires fracturing the rock, a technique called "fracking." The method has raised concern about damage to underground water supplies and faces opposition from environmental groups, especially in areas that do not now have oil and gas drilling.

Somewhat like oil, natural gas deposits are disproportionately concentrated in the Middle East. Natural gas can be chilled until it turns into a liquid and then shipped by tanker, and the American capacity to import such gas has grown, but a long supply chain for natural gas could come to represent another energy vulnerability, the report said.

Dash for Gas Raises Environmental Worries

BY KATE GALBRAITH | JULY 12, 2010

FORT WORTH, TEXAS — American politicians often extol natural gas as abundant, cleaner-burning than other fossil fuels, and domestically produced, unlike Middle Eastern oil. But the process of extracting it is raising concerns among people with wells in their backyards.

Anger and fear were on display last week at a public meeting convened by the U.S. Environmental Protection Agency in Fort Worth, a gas-drilling hub. Dozens of local residents took turns at the microphone to voice concerns about potential contamination of drinking water.

A film called "Gasland," released last month on the cable channel HBO, showed people in drilling areas lighting their tap water on fire, as gas found its way into their water supply.

"I am frustrated and angry," said State Representative Lon Burnam, Democrat of Fort Worth, who spoke at the meeting and decried the "inadequacies" of state regulators.

At issue is a procedure known as hydraulic fracturing, or fracking, which has been adopted widely in the United States over the past 10 years to extract gas trapped in shale formations. It is just starting to spread to other parts of the world, including Europe, China and Australia.

Fracking involves shooting a mixture of water, sand and chemicals deep underground, to break up rock and release the gas. The technique has vastly expanded access to shale-gas reserves in the United States, including deposits in Pennsylvania, New York, Texas and Louisiana.

More than 20,000 wells of this nature have been drilled in the past 10 years, according to a study of natural gas released last month by the Massachusetts Institute of Technology. (Natural gas accounts for 23 percent of U.S. electricity generation, and a number of politicians are calling for increased use of the fuel in vehicles.)

In Europe and Asia, large-scale recovery of shale gas is likely to happen within 10 years, according to Amy M. Jaffe, the director of the Baker Institute Energy Forum at Rice University in Houston.

Poland, for example, is "already tendering for exploration of shale gas," she said. Canada is also speeding up its shale development, Ms. Jaffe said.

The industry said it operated far below aquifer levels, so fracking would do no harm to water. Hydraulic fracturing is a "safe, proven technology that has been used over one million times over 60 years," Angie Burckhalter, the vice president of regulatory affairs for the Oklahoma Independent Petroleum Association, said at the Fort Worth meeting.

But people with homes in the gas fields increasingly dispute that.

Tim Ruggiero, a Texas resident who also spoke at the meeting, said that after drilling began near his home, a test on his water turned up an unknown substance that resembled MTBE, a gasoline additive.

In New York, state officials are moving aggressively to protect the watershed supplying New York City with drinking water from potential contamination from hydraulic fracturing.

Part of the problem, according to environmentalists, is that gas companies do not disclose at the wellheads what chemicals they are using. They also argue that regulations, which in the United States are mostly the responsibility of state governments rather than the national government, tend to be weak — especially in drilling-friendly places like Texas.

On the national level, the industry obtained an explicit exemption for hydraulic fracturing from a key provision of the Safe Drinking Water Act, as part of 2005 energy legislation.

Hydraulic fracturing requires an immense amount of water, another concern in water-constrained regions.

The experience of the United States may foreshadow that of other parts of the world. Europe, for example, would love to reduce its dependence on natural gas from Russia, and discussions about exploring for shale-gas reserves are taking place in Germany, Hungary and Romania, as well as Poland.

There is a lot of talk about a "dash for gas" in Europe, said Mark Walker, a London-based energy partner in the law firm Allen & Overy. New sources of generation are needed to meet growing demand for electricity, he said, especially as old coal or nuclear plants reach the end of their life or get shut down because of European environmental legislation, particularly in the case of coal.

Companies like Exxon Mobil, ConocoPhillips, Marathon Oil and Chevron have already signed or negotiated for deals in Poland to explore shale deposits.

The U.S. government is encouraging their efforts, through research partnerships with other countries. Last November, President Barack Obama and President Hu Jintao of China announced a U.S.-China Shale Gas Resource Initiative, aimed at promoting "environmentally sustainable development of shale gas resources" and doing joint technical studies.

A similar initiative was just formed with Poland.

As American companies begin scouting for shale-gas overseas, the regulatory environment for hydraulic fracturing at home seems poised to tighten, especially in the wake of the BP oil spill in the Gulf of Mexico, which has increased public skepticism about the oil and gas industry's safety assurances.

The Environmental Protection Agency, at the request of Congress, is about to start studying the effects of fracking on groundwater; initial findings should be ready by late 2012.

The purpose of the meeting in Fort Worth last week was to hear feedback from the public about the study; a similar meeting is be held Tuesday in Denver, followed by two more, in Pennsylvania and New York.

Ms. Jaffe of the Baker Institute said that gas companies were developing nontoxic drilling fluids. She suggested the adoption of policies that would take away drilling licenses from companies shown to have "negligent disposal procedures" for water used in the drilling process.

Last week, Timothy Wirth, the president of the United Nations Foundation and a former senator from Colorado, told the Colorado Oil and Gas Association that while natural gas remained a crucial fuel, the regulatory status quo must change.

"Responsible regulation rewards the good performers and weeds out the bad — and that is a good thing for any industry," Mr. Wirth said.

More regulation cannot come soon enough for some Texans.

"When is E.P.A. going to quit with these meetings and roll up its sleeves and get to work?" asked Robert Snoke, the head of a neighborhood association in Fort Worth, at the meeting last week.

E.P.A. to Study Chemicals Used to Tap Natural Gas

BY TOM ZELLER JR. | SEPT. 9, 2010

THE ENVIRONMENTAL PROTECTION AGENCY sent letters to nine drilling companies on Thursday requesting detailed information about the chemicals contained in fluids used to crack open underground rock formations in the hunt for oil and natural gas.

The move is part of the federal agency's preparations for a long-term scientific study of the effects of the practice, known as hydraulic fracturing or "fracking," on drinking water and public health.

"Natural gas is an important part of our nation's energy future, and it's critical that the extraction of this valuable natural resource does not come at the expense of safe water and healthy communities," the E.P.A. administrator, Lisa P. Jackson, said in a statement.

The agency asked the companies to respond to its request within seven days and to voluntarily provide the information within 30 days, according to a copy of the letter provided by the agency.

"To the extent that E.P.A. does not receive sufficient data in response to this letter," the agency warned, "E.P.A. will be exploring legal alternatives to compel submission of the needed information."

Hydraulic fracturing has been used for decades, and the industry maintains that it is safe. But in recent years, environmental groups and community activists, pointing to inconclusive but sometimes compelling anecdotes of possible water contamination, have complained that the drilling practice is far too loosely regulated. Those complaints increased after the BP oil spill in the Gulf of Mexico.

In a 2004 study, the E.P.A. concluded that hydraulic fracturing was essentially safe, but critics quickly condemned that analysis as sloppy and politically motivated. Congress used that study as partial justification the following year to exempt hydraulic fracturing from regulation under the Safe Drinking Water Act.

FRED R. CONRAD/THE NEW YORK TIMES

A drilling rig in Dimock, Pa., where hydraulic fracturing is being used to tap natural gas reserves in the Marcellus shale formation.

The current Congress passed legislation requiring the E.P.A. to re-examine the issue, and the agency is currently drafting a new study with an aim of publishing results by the end of 2012.

Most companies that make the fluids used in hydraulic fracturing have declined to disclose their formulas, arguing that the exact components are trade secrets.

Cathy G. Mann, a spokeswoman for Halliburton, one of those named in the E.P.A.'s announcement, said the company had not yet received the official request for data, but that it planned to fully cooperate with the agency.

"Halliburton supports and continues to comply with state, local and federal requirements promoting the forthright disclosure of the chemical additives that typically comprise less than one-half of 1 percent of our hydraulic fracturing solutions," Ms. Mann said by e-mail. "We view this both as a means of enhancing public safety, and as a way to engage the public in a straightforward manner."

In addition to Halliburton, the E.P.A. said that letters were sent to BJ Services, Complete Production Services, Key Energy Services, Patterson-UTI Energy, RPC Inc., Schlumberger, Superior Well Services and Weatherford International.

Stephanie Meadows, the upstream senior policy adviser for the American Petroleum Institute, a trade group representing oil and natural gas companies, took issue with the threat of legal action for noncompliance.

"I'm not sure how they would do that, or if they even have the authority to do that," she said. "I'm little disappointed with the threats, because I thought we'd made it clear all along that we want to be helpful."

The oil and natural gas industry has long maintained that hydraulic fracturing fluids are almost entirely a mixture of sand and water, with just trace amounts of chemical lubricants, thickeners and other compounds. None of the compounds come in contact with the water table, the industry says.

An E.P.A. spokeswoman said the agency would honor the companies' requests for confidentiality about their exact formulas unless it determined that "disclosure of the information is necessary to protect health or the environment against an unreasonable risk of injury."

The industry estimates that 90 percent of the more than 450,000 operating natural gas wells in the United States rely on hydraulic fracturing.

As part of its information gathering, the agency is also asking the companies to turn over any data they have on the potential health and environmental effects of hydraulic fracturing, information on the location of all sites where it has been practiced and the procedures for its use.

The E.P.A. has been conducting a series of public hearings on hydraulic fracturing, which has become a controversial topic in Pennsylvania, West Virginia and parts of western New York, where potentially huge reserves of previously unreachable natural gas have drilling companies angling for access.

Two days of hearings are scheduled to be held next week in Binghamton, N.Y. Organizers expect large crowds and major demonstrations both for and against natural gas development in the state.

The New York State Senate overwhelmingly passed a bill that would block natural gas exploration using hydraulic fracturing until early next year, to allow for closer examination of its effects. The State Assembly is expected to take up the matter later this month.

In Europe, the Promise and Fears of a New Fuel

BY BETH GARDINER | FEB. 22, 2011

LONDON — Energy companies across Europe are probing the ground for natural gas trapped in shale rock, hoping to replicate an American boom that has given consumers in the United States a major new supply of affordable fuel.

In countries like Britain, Germany and Poland, exploratory drilling is under way, or about to begin, as engineers try to determine how much shale gas is present and how easy it will be to retrieve. New technologies for extracting natural gas from stone have raised worries about contamination of drinking water while also driving a huge drilling expansion in the United States, helping push prices down by two thirds since 2008 and reducing dependence on imports.

Shale gas production accounted for 14 percent of U.S. natural gas production in 2009 and is expected to reach 45 percent by 2035, the U.S. Energy Information Agency estimates.

"It was an amazing story in the U.S., this very rapid increase in the availability of shale gas," said Paul Stevens, senior research fellow for energy at Chatham House, a London research institute. European exploration has big potential too, he added, but "the problem is there are a great many barriers to converting that potential into actual molecules of gas."

It is far too early to know how much extraction will be possible in Europe, said Mr. Stevens and other analysts. Hurdles in Europe, Mr. Stevens said, include technical issues like the size, depth and clay content of European shale fields; environmental regulations, which are generally tighter than in the United States; and the Continent's higher population density.

"I would guess it will eventually happen, but I think it's going to be a lot slower than a lot of people are guessing," he said. "It is not going to be the sort of spectacular change we've seen in the United States."

The five-year-old American boom has been driven by technologies including horizontal underground drilling and hydraulic fracturing, known as "fracking," which uses high-intensity spraying of water, sand and chemicals to break up stone hundreds, or even thousands, of meters beneath the surface.

The Oscar-nominated documentary "Gasland" has highlighted worries about the practice's environmental effect, particularly fears that fracking fluids and contaminated water are poisoning nearby aquifers. New York, home along with Pennsylvania and West Virginia to the rich Marcellus Shale, has temporarily halted some drilling while it assesses environmental risks. The U.S. Environmental Protection Agency plans to release initial results of a review on fracking next year.

Many in Europe share such worries. France recently halted drilling, pending an environmental study. In the British House of Commons, the Energy and Climate Change Committee is holding an inquiry on shale gas exploration, which it estimates could eventually meet 10 percent of the country's needs.

But with much of the Continent dependent on Russia for natural gas supplies, politicians and regulators are likely to be tempted by a reliable new source, and big energy companies like Exxon Mobil are already staking their claims. While American finds — estimated by the U.S. government at 827 trillion cubic feet, or 23.4 trillion cubic meters, enough for an estimated 36 years — are so big, they have turned anxiety about dependence on imports into hopes of becoming a natural gas exporter, European reserves are likely to meet only a small slice of the Continent's energy needs.

"The amounts would not transform the whole of the energy situation. It would not take over," said Brian Horsfield, director of GASH, an industry-financed shale gas research project. "But it's a bargaining chip, it's a component of the energy mix, and it's good to have some energy under your own feet."

It will take three to five years for the scale of Europe's shale gas potential to become clear, and technological advances may ease some environmental concerns in the meantime, he said.

With global temperatures rising, some say that pursuing new sources of fossil fuels is a recipe for disaster.

If there is any hope of keeping global temperature increases to 2 degrees Celsius (3.6 Fahrenheit), as world leaders promised at the 2009 Copenhagen climate meeting, "then the math shows there is no space left for shale gas, or for that matter for other fossil fuels, but you certainly wouldn't add another one to the mix," said Kevin Anderson, a professor at the Tyndall Center for Climate Change at the University of Manchester in England.

"I think there will be a big push for it — this is the petrochemical industry, there's always a big push," Mr. Anderson added. "We're all locked into fossil fuels, they are hugely influential in terms of government, employment, tax revenues. We've got to move off that in a time frame we can hardly imagine."

Studies Say Natural Gas Has Its Own Environmental Problems

BY TOM ZELLER JR. | APRIL 11, 2011

NATURAL GAS, WITH its reputation as a linchpin in the effort to wean the nation off dirtier fossil fuels and reduce global warming, may not be as clean over all as its proponents say.

Even as natural gas production in the United States increases and Washington gives it a warm embrace as a crucial component of America's energy future, two coming studies try to poke holes in the clean-and-green reputation of natural gas. They suggest that the rush to develop the nation's vast, unconventional sources of natural gas is logistically impractical and likely to do more to heat up the planet than mining and burning coal.

The problem, the studies suggest, is that planet-warming methane, the chief component of natural gas, is escaping into the atmosphere in far larger quantities than previously thought, with as much as 7.9 percent of it puffing out from shale gas wells, intentionally vented or flared, or seeping from loose pipe fittings along gas distribution lines. This offsets natural gas's most important advantage as an energy source: it burns cleaner than other fossil fuels and releases lower carbon dioxide emissions.

"The old dogma of natural gas being better than coal in terms of greenhouse gas emissions gets stated over and over without qualification," said Robert Howarth, a professor of ecology and environmental biology at Cornell University and the lead author of one of the studies. Mr. Howarth said his analysis, which looked specifically at methane leakage rates in unconventional shale gas development, was among the first of its kind and that much more research was needed.

"I don't think this is the end of the story," said Mr. Howarth, who is an opponent of growing gas development in western New York. "I think this is just the beginning of the story, and before governments and the industry push ahead on gas development, at the very least we ought to do a better job of making measurements."

The findings are certain to stir debate. For much of the last decade, the natural gas industry has carefully cultivated a green reputation, often with the help of environmental groups that embrace the resource as a clean-burning "bridge fuel" to a renewable energy future. The industry argues that it has vastly reduced the amount of fugitive methane with new technologies and upgraded pipe fittings and other equipment.

Mark D. Whitley, a senior vice president for engineering and technology with Range Resources, a gas drilling company with operations in several regions of the country, said the losses suggested by Mr. Howarth's study were simply too high.

"These are huge numbers," he said. "That the industry would let what amounts to trillions of cubic feet of gas get away from us doesn't make any sense. That's not the business that we're in."

Natural gas is already the principal source of heat in half of American households. Advocates like the former oil tycoon T. Boone Pickens have also long sought to promote it as a substitute for coal in electricity generation or gasoline in a new generation of natural gas cars. And the development of new ways to tap reserves of natural gas means production is likely to increase sharply.

Two weeks ago, President Obama included natural gas in his vision for America. Clark Stevens, a White House spokesman, said that the administration's energy priorities were not about picking one energy source over another, but about diversifying the nation's energy mix. "This process will continue to be based on the best science available to ensure our energy sources, including our nation's natural gas reserves, are developed safely and responsibly," Mr. Stevens said on Friday.

The ability to pull natural gas economically from previously inaccessible formations deep underground has made huge quantities of the resource available in wide areas of the country, including Texas, Louisiana, Pennsylvania, New York, Wyoming and Colorado.

KEVIN MOLONEY FOR THE NEW YORK TIMES

A natural gas pipeline in Colorado.

Such unconventional gas production accounts for nearly a quarter of total production in the United States, according to the latest figures from the Energy Information Administration. That is expected to reach 45 percent by 2035.

But the cleanliness of natural gas is largely based on its lower carbon dioxide emissions when burned. It emits roughly half the amount of carbon dioxide as coal and about 30 percent less than oil.

Less clear, largely because no one has bothered to look, are the emissions over its entire production life cycle — that is, from the moment a well is plumbed to the point at which the gas is used.

Methane leaks have long been a concern because while methane dissipates in the atmosphere more quickly than carbon dioxide, it is far more efficient at trapping heat. Recent evidence has suggested that the amount of leakage has been underestimated. A report in January by the nonprofit journalism organization ProPublica, for example, noted that the Environmental Protection Agency had recently doubled its estimates for the amount of methane that is vented or lost from natural gas distribution lines.

Chris Tucker, a spokesman for Energy in Depth, a coalition of independent oil and natural gas producers, dismissed Mr. Howarth as an advocate who is opposed to hydraulic-fracturing or “fracking,” a practice associated with unconventional gas development involving the high-pressure injection of water, sand and chemicals deep underground to break up shale formations and release gas deposits. Mr. Howarth said his credentials as a scientist spoke for themselves.

Mr. Howarth included methane losses associated with flow-back and drill-out processes in hydraulic fracturing and other unconventional gas drilling techniques.

The study combined these emissions with studies of other methane losses along the processing and distribution cycle to arrive at an estimated total methane loss range from 3.6 to 7.9 percent for the shale gas industry.

The researchers include a recent study from the Goddard Institute for Space Studies at NASA suggesting that an interaction of methane with certain aerosol particles significantly amplifies methane’s already potent greenhouse gas effects, particularly over a 20-year time horizon. When all is factored together, Mr. Howarth and his colleagues conclude that the greenhouse gas footprint of shale gas can be as much as 20 percent greater than, and perhaps twice as high as, coal per unit of energy.

David Hughes, a geoscientist and research fellow at the Post Carbon Institute, an energy and climate research organization in California, used Mr. Howarth’s research as part of a broader look at natural gas as a substitute for coal in electricity generation and oil in transportation.

Mr. Hughes’s full report is scheduled to be released in May, but in a draft version shared with The New York Times, Mr. Hughes suggested that while natural gas would play an important role in the nation’s energy mix, both cases were practical impossibilities.

"I think it's going to be very challenging, to put it mildly, to ramp up shale gas production by fourfold, which is the federal government's projection for 2035," Mr. Hughes said. "I'm not saying it can't be done, but if it was done, the amount of drilling you're looking at to make that happen is staggering."

Mr. Hughes, using Mr. Howarth's calculations, also concludes that replacing coal with natural gas for base load electricity production will most likely make greenhouse gas emissions worse. It would be better, he argues, to improve energy efficiency, rely on natural gas in niche vehicle markets and balance continued construction of wind and solar power to produce electricity.

David Hawkins, the director of climate programs with the Natural Resources Defense Council, said that much could be done by regulators to nudge drillers to capture more of the fugitive methane, but that it is often more economical for industry to simply let it escape.

Mr. Hawkins also said that too little was known about just how much methane was being lost and vented, and that studies like Mr. Howarth's, while needed, relied on too slim a data set to be considered the final word.

"This is a huge and growing industry, and we just don't have the information we need to make sure that this resource is being developed as cleanly as it can be," Mr. Hawkins said.

"We view his shining a flashlight into this dark closet to be a service," Mr. Hawkins added, "but the flashlight is still a dim one, and we still can't see everything in the closet."

In North Dakota, Flames of Wasted Natural Gas Light the Prairie

BY CLIFFORD KRAUSS | SEPT. 26, 2011

NEW TOWN, N.D. — Across western North Dakota, hundreds of fires rise above fields of wheat and sunflowers and bales of hay. At night, they illuminate the prairie skies like giant fireflies.

They are not wildfires caused by lightning strikes or other acts of nature, but the deliberate burning of natural gas by oil companies rushing to extract oil from the Bakken shale field and take advantage of the high price of crude. The gas bubbles up alongside the far more valuable oil, and with less economic incentive to capture it, the drillers treat the gas as waste and simply burn it.

Every day, more than 100 million cubic feet of natural gas is flared this way — enough energy to heat half a million homes for a day.

The flared gas also spews at least two million tons of carbon dioxide into the atmosphere every year, as much as 384,000 cars or a medium-size coal-fired power plant would emit, alarming some environmentalists.

All told, 30 percent of the natural gas produced in North Dakota is burned as waste. No other major domestic oil field currently flares close to that much, though the practice is still common in countries like Russia, Nigeria and Iran.

With few government regulations that limit the flaring, more burning is also taking place in the Eagle Ford shale field in Texas, and some environmentalists and industry executives say that it could happen in Oklahoma, Arkansas and Ohio, too, as drilling expands in new fields there unlocked by techniques like hydraulic fracturing and horizontal drilling.

"North Dakota is not as bad as Kazakhstan, but this is not what you would expect a civilized, efficient society to do: to flare off a perfectly good product just because it's expensive to bring to market," said

Michael E. Webber, associate director of the Center for International Energy and Environmental Policy at the University of Texas at Austin.

The oil companies say economic reality is driving the flaring in the Bakken, the biggest oil field discovered in the United States in four decades. They argue that they cannot afford to pay for pipelines and processing plants to capture and sell the gas until they actually drill oil wells and calculate how much gas will bubble out of the oil. And reinjection of the carbon dioxide, commonly done in conventional oil fields, is more difficult and expensive in less permeable shale fields.

"This field covers 15,000 square miles, so it takes time to go and test what's there and then build a gathering system and plant," said Harold G. Hamm, chief executive of Continental Resources, one of the biggest oil producers in the Bakken.

The widespread flaring is a step backward for a domestic energy industry. Most oil and gas fields in the United States have well-developed facilities to gather and process gas.

But the recent rise of shale drilling has changed the economic calculus. Natural gas prices have plunged since 2008 as vast shale fields laden with gas are tapped through hydraulic fracturing and horizontal drilling. Meanwhile, those same techniques have opened up other shale fields rich with oil.

With oil prices high amid strong global demand and leases as short as five years for land in the Bakken, drillers have found it more profitable to just grab the oil and burn the gas. Building out the infrastructure to handle gas would substantially raise costs and slow development, and efforts so far to use the gas for electrical generation have had limited success because it contains components that burn too hot.

"I'll tell you why people flare: It's cheap," said Troy Anderson, lead operator of a North Dakota gas-processing plant owned by Whiting Petroleum. "Pipelines are expensive: You have to maintain them. You need permits to build them. They are a pain."

JIM WILSON/THE NEW YORK TIMES

Thirty percent of the natural gas extracted in North Dakota is flared off, like this gas near Ray.

Although capturing the gas is the best option, scientists say that flaring is better for the environment than venting the gas into the atmosphere. Pure natural gas is mostly methane, which has far greater heat-trapping qualities than carbon dioxide.

Regulations on flaring are loose in North Dakota, as they are in most states, and there are no current federal regulations on flaring at oil and gas wells. That is largely because flaring has not been a significant concern since the 1970s, when the federal government insisted that oil companies re-inject gas into Alaska's North Slope rather than flare it.

So far, North Dakota health officials say that flaring has not produced any serious air pollution problems. But flaring could eventually become another environmental headache for an industry already under attack over concerns that hydraulic fracturing, also known as fracking, could jeopardize water quality.

JIM WILSON/THE NEW YORK TIMES

Bill Herrmann of Whiting Petroleum looking at a section of 24-inch gas pipe for a line the company is building.

The federal Environmental Protection Agency has recently proposed new air emissions standards for fracked wells, and it has also begun to ask oil companies to compile data on greenhouse gas emissions from drilling and other operations.

"One day a regulator is going to say, 'I'm not going to give you one more permit until you tell me what you are going to do with the gas,' " said Charif Souki, chief executive of Cheniere Energy, who hopes to eventually export the excess gas in liquefied form.

Environmentalists are also beginning to express alarm. "It's time for the regulators to take a hard look at the impacts of flaring and make sure that available solutions to the flaring problem are required before there is any further widespread expansion of the practice," said Amy Mall, senior policy analyst at the Natural Resources Defense Council. Some of the companies working in North Dakota, including Whiting, are investing $3 billion over the next three years in pipelines and several large processing plants to deliver gas to Midwest markets rather than burn it.

Whiting, a Colorado company that was one of the early explorers in the Bakken, sees particular value in the gas found here because it contains large amounts of propane and butane that it can extract and sell at a profit in addition to the gas itself.

The company is rapidly expanding oil drilling while building and expanding two plants to process its own gas as well as gas produced by others. Whiting was flaring 80 percent of the gas in its first major Bakken field in 2007, but says it has now reduced its flaring to 20 percent across all fields, which will fall further when its second gas plant comes online.

"Our goal is to have zero emissions," said James T. Brown, Whiting's president and chief operating officer. "It's a waste to be wasting all of this energy."

While the projects by Whiting and others could reduce flaring over the next two years, some executives acknowledge that it will be a continuing problem as the industry increases the number of wells in the area from 5,000 to a projected 48,000 over the next 20 years.

Wayde Schafer, the Sierra Club's North Dakota conservation organizer, said that the industry needed to slow down development if it could not protect the air. "You can do it fast or you can do it right," he said.

A White-Hot Future for Oil and Gas

BY JAMES KANTER | OCT. 10, 2011

BRUSSELS — Opportunities in oil and natural gas have rarely been so bountiful. New finds and technological advances and fresh access to some countries are pushing exploration and production into areas once considered peripheral.

Some of the most promising new fields are in deep water off the coast of Brazil. Experts say they could yield as much oil as the North Sea. There have been significant strikes off the coast of French Guiana, north of Brazil, and off Ghana in West Africa.

Iraq is opening up after years of sanctions and war. It could be a second Saudi Arabia.

Russia is increasing production in its Arctic regions, while Canada is steadily producing more oil from its abundant tar sands.

In the United States, the vast deposits of natural gas found in shale rock could transform the country into a major energy exporter.

Those prospects "will certainly have significant impacts on the energy map," said Maria van der Hoeven, the newly appointed executive director of the International Energy Agency, which advises member countries, including Germany, Japan and the United States, on energy policy.

The prospects are coming into view as revolution and instability threaten new investments in resource-rich countries like Libya and Iraq and after a nuclear disaster at the Fukushima Daiichi power plant in Japan that prompted Germany to declare it would phase out nuclear technology.

Fewer reactors should drastically increase demand for electricity from natural gas, while lower-than-expected growth in energy exports from the Middle East and North Africa could "radically alter the global energy balance," Ms. van der Hoeven said.

Yet the new opportunities also present companies and investors with a dizzying array of risks — including the high cost of development and exploitation and the possibility that energy prices could fall, especially if the global economy slows drastically and energy demand slackens.

"Quite a few bets are off, if prices drop too far," said Herman T. Franssen, a senior director at Energy Intelligence, a research company that organizes the annual Oil & Money conference with the International Herald Tribune.

Mr. Franssen said oil and natural gas prices would need to remain at relatively high levels to pay for exploration and production in increasingly demanding environments, which produce their own technological risks.

Petrobras, the state-run company leading the deepwater venture in Brazil, is "adding a major challenge on top of a major challenge" by drilling through 2 kilometers, or 1.2 miles, of salt to gain access to oil, said Mark Moody-Stuart, a former chairman of Royal Dutch Shell.

"Salt moves, dissolves and shears away, and it's highly corrosive," Mr. Moody-Stuart said. "That kind of drilling worried me in the past, and it worries me now as we head ever deeper."

Those factors make wells more time-consuming and expensive to complete, but they are no more likely to lead to accidents than conditions at other deepwater drilling sites, Mr. Moody-Stuart said.

Of course, since a well blowout destroyed a rig operated by BP last year, spilling huge amounts of crude oil into the Gulf of Mexico, concerns have grown about whether companies take enough precautions in increasingly extreme conditions.

It was months before BP devised a way to stanch the leak, and the ability of the U.S. government to manage its oil industry was questioned.

"How do we consider similar scenarios, as operators push increasingly complex projects in West Africa, Brazil and the Arctic?" asked Paul Sheng, the director for oil and natural gas at McKinsey, a consulting firm, referring to the Gulf of Mexico accident.

By comparison, he said, the "resources and technology were available readily in the U.S. to respond."

Stricter safety controls and higher caps on liability making it harder to obtain insurance could drive smaller companies out of the market. But large international oil companies would be affected too.

An increasing proportion of their portfolio comes from unconventional sources and deepwater drilling since national oil companies began taking far greater control of the most accessible and productive oil fields at the end of the 1970s — a trend that has continued.

The squeeze on international oil companies has been conspicuous in Russia, where Royal Dutch Shell was forced to sell half of its $20 billion Sakhalin II oil and natural gas deepwater development to the state natural gas company, Gazprom, in 2007.

Last month, the offices of BP's Russian venture were raided as part of a long-running feud with powerful Russian shareholders.

Even so, foreign investors are becoming increasingly savvy at navigating the treacherous Russian business environment, bankers said. Exxon Mobil structured its recent deal in the Russian Arctic — which appears to supersede an earlier deal involving BP — in ways that avoided earlier pitfalls, they said.

Much of the bullishness about future demand for additional resources is based on the growth of China.

Most Saudi-exported oil already goes to East Asia — a boon for Saudi Aramco, which still manages some of the world's largest crude oil reserves, at a time when the state-owned Saudi company's traditional Western customers aspire to greater self-sufficiency.

But in a rapidly and drastically shifting geopolitical and economic order, reliance on China presents risks too.

"Question No. 1 is, What happens if China ends up helping Iran confront the West by helping develop its oil fields?" said Ghassan Salamé, dean of the Paris School of International Affairs at Sciences Po.

"The new function of Middle Eastern oil will almost certainly be as a major bargaining chip in the relationship between the United States and China," he said.

For now, strong economic growth has given the Chinese "tremendous ability to invest in new supplies, both at home and abroad, so they are helping supplies to keep pace with demand, which aids market stability," said Ms. van der Hoeven of the I.E.A.

She also lauded the "continued building of strategic oil stocks" by China as "a significant contribution to the global capacity to respond to supply emergencies."

Another reason for stable prices is that demand from emerging economies may offset any prolonged slowdown in the West, said Fereidun Fesharaki, the chief executive of FACTS Global Energy, a consulting group based in Singapore.

On the other side of the energy equation, Saudi Arabia and other powerful low-cost producers in the Middle East are focused on keeping the price of oil at more than $80 a barrel to fund job creation and better social welfare at home and to support poorer states in the region, said Mr. Franssen of Energy Intelligence.

With oil expected to stay at robust levels, the producing countries once considered to be on the periphery of the global industry are racing to build their economies by maximizing foreign earnings from oil and natural gas.

But perhaps in no country are the perils, as well as the possibilities, more apparent than in Iraq.

A number of oil fields are still mined, and the country's lack of infrastructure means that getting oil to foreign markets is a challenge. Iraq could also explode into renewed conflict, particularly if relations worsen between Baghdad and the Kurdish authorities in the north, where some of the largest reserves are located.

International oil companies still must settle how much money to contribute toward a multibillion-dollar water injection facility that is vital to regulating the pressure of reservoirs. "There are wild expectations, but Iraq is not Saudi Arabia," said Issam al-Chalabi, a former minister of oil in Iraq who left the country 20 years ago. "There may be huge amounts of oil, but getting it out requires two things Iraq hasn't got, which are stability and expertise."

Those hazards — and the possibility that Iraq will need to lower targets because of market conditions or under pressure from OPEC — have pushed international oil companies to seek deals with Baghdad that guarantee payment of their fees even when supply is disrupted, according to Mr. Chalabi.

Still, oil company executives appear sanguine.

Robert Dudley, the chief executive of BP, which is developing the vast Rumaila field in Iraq with China National Petroleum, said last month that the goal of producing 2.85 million barrels a day by 2017 was attainable and that there was no need for any change to contracts.

Mr. Chalabi predicted that the Iraqi government would have to lower its production estimates by the end of the year, probably to about 6 million barrels a day by 2017, from current estimates of about 13 million barrels a day.

That could mean that BP would eventually lower its production forecasts as well.

Libya, an important supplier of the sweet crude oil that many refineries around the world depend on, also presents challenges.

Its Transitional National Council could demand revisions to deals made with the old regime if it decides that pricing terms are too low or if contracts are tainted by corruption.

Any such allegations would be a particularly sensitive matter in the United States, where the government is putting the finishing touches on transparency rules requiring companies to publish what they pay to host countries.

Such risks in the developing world have helped to make Canada, with its stable legal system and proximity to U.S. consumers, an increasingly enticing option for many companies.

Canada has some of the largest known oil reserves — in the form of bitumen — outside of Saudi Arabia and is producing 1.8 million barrels per day from oil sands, or twice the amount it was producing in 2003, said Murray D. Smith, a former minister of energy for Alberta, the province where the industry is based.

"We see technology making the unconventional resource the conventional source in a lot of places, and nowhere is that more true than in Canada," said Mr. Smith, who serves on the boards of two companies with stakes in the industry.

Yet even this vast resource is not immune to risk.

The European Union still is deciding whether to modify a law on transport fuels to penalize oil sands crude, which emits more greenhouse gases than conventional crude, partly because it requires more processing.

In the United States there have been large protests against plans to build a 1,660-mile pipeline called Keystone XL from Alberta to Texas. The protesters say tar sands crude is more corrosive than conventional crude and poses unique dangers to aquifers along the pipeline route.

The project is awaiting final approval from the U.S. State Department and could face legal challenges from environmental groups.

Another unconventional resource that has drawn huge interest from investors — and environmentalists — is shale gas.

In the past decade companies like Devon Energy, with large operations in Texas, proved it was possible to extract gas from sites that other companies assumed were exhausted by drilling into nearby areas where gas was trapped in rock formations.

The rapid emergence of new techniques led the I.E.A. to estimate this year that shale gas — together with other unconventional forms like tight gas trapped in hard rocks, and coal-bed methane found in coal seams or surrounding rock — made up half the recoverable gas resources worldwide, or enough to last 120 years at current rates of consumption.

(Annual global gas consumption is expected to increase 37 percent from 2010 to 2035 to reach 4.535 trillion cubic meters, according to the I.E.A.)

Oil and gas majors have been racing to catch up, though cost could become a limiting factor.

"A lot of money is being spent on land and wells, but there's a high probability of economic failure," said Thomas S. Ahlbrandt, a former senior official at the U.S. Geological Survey credited with numerous oil and gas discoveries. "Drilling these wells can cost around $10 million a pop, and you've got to have the know-how to hit the sweet spot," he said.

There also are questions about how rapidly the industry will grow elsewhere.

In France, the lower house of Parliament voted in May to ban "fracking" — the use of highly pressurized water, sand and chemicals deep underground to loosen shale gas — on environmental grounds.

The authorities in South Africa were among those that imposed moratoriums on the technique this year.

But as other countries explore low-carbon options beyond nuclear energy, many, like Poland, will look to their huge domestic reserves of shale gas to lessen their reliance on burning comparatively polluting coal.

And for those countries determined to increase the amount of power they generate from renewable sources, tapping more gas from shale could help provide the energy needed to compensate for the intermittency of the wind and sun.

Renewable energy "almost always needs to be supplemented by other fuels," said Mr. Franssen of Energy Intelligence. "One of the best answers is using renewables and gas together," he said, "and you can bet shale gas will become a significant part of that mix in some places."

Natural Gas Signals a 'Manufacturing Renaissance'

BY JIM MOTAVALLI | APRIL 10, 2012

AS HORIZONTAL DRILLING and the controversial extraction technique known as fracking have made domestically produced natural gas more available and sharply cheaper, that gas has been widely embraced by industry, electric utilities and trucking fleets.

The rapid development of shale gas technology has helped reduce energy imports and, in some cases, encouraged companies producing petrochemicals, steel, fertilizers and other products to return to the United States after relocating overseas. Natural gas exports are growing and terminals built to hold imported supplies are being repurposed for international sales.

The American petrochemical industry, for example, uses natural gas as both its primary raw material, in the form of liquid ethane, and as an energy fuel. And cheaper prices have led to a major expansion of capacity in the United States.

The hydrocarbon molecules in natural gas are split apart and then recombined as building blocks for many products, including bulk chemicals and fertilizers. The chemical ethylene, which is largely derived from natural gas, is used to make things like pool liners, building insulation and food packaging.

According to Kevin Swift, chief economist at the American Chemistry Council, European producers mostly use oil-derived raw materials for making these same products. "The U.S. has a competitive advantage when oil is seven times as expensive as natural gas, but now we have more like a 50-to-1 advantage," he said. "The 'shale gale' is really driving this. A million B.T.U.'s of natural gas that might cost $11 in Europe and $14 in South Korea is $2.25 in the U.S. Partly because of that, chemical producers have plans to expand ethylene capacity in the U.S. by more than 25 percent between now and 2017."

MICHAEL F. MCELROY FOR THE NEW YORK TIMES

Clean Energy in partnership with Pilot Travel Centers opened up a liquid natural gas truck filling station in Seville, Ohio.

A 2011 PricewaterhouseCoopers study estimates that high rates of shale gas recovery could result in a million new manufacturing jobs by 2025. Robert McCutcheon, United States industrial products leader at PricewaterhouseCoopers, said in a statement that the revived natural gas industry "has the potential to spark a manufacturing renaissance in the U.S., including billions in cost savings, a significant number of new jobs and a greater investment in U.S. plants."

The growing commitment to natural gas faces some headwinds because of continuing concern over the safety of fracking, which involves forcing pressurized fluids into shale formations to fracture the rock and release the gas deposits.

Some environmentalists say that fracking can cause drinking water to become contaminated with chemicals and released methane, which is a powerful naturally occurring greenhouse gas and the primary ingredient in natural gas. Other complaints tie the disposal of fracking wastewater to a series of small earthquakes. Some states and municipalities with questions about fracking have imposed temporary moratoriums on the extraction technique.

Despite these issues, natural gas is expanding its reach in manufacturing. The Nucor Corporation, which makes direct-reduced iron in a process heavily reliant on natural gas, said in 2010 that it would build a $750 million facility in Louisiana. In 2004, the company dismantled a similar Louisiana plant and shipped it to Trinidad.

According to Nucor, affordable domestic natural gas means its made-in-Louisiana direct-reduced iron, which is sold in pellet or briquette form as a raw material for steel mills, can be delivered at the same price as the product shipped from Trinidad. "Affordable American shale gas has completely changed the economics for us," said Katherine Miller, a Nucor spokeswoman.

Methanex, a Canadian company that makes methanol from natural gas is planning to move a plant from Chile to Louisiana, with production to begin in 2014. Gary Rowan, a Methanex vice president, said that his company had also shut down a Louisiana plant in the early 2000s. "Certainly, the outlook for low North American natural gas prices is one of the reasons we selected Louisiana as a new location for our methanol plant," he said.

Electric utilities see a significant natural gas price advantage over other fuels, but because of pending and potential environmental regulations they are also motivated by its status as the fossil fuel with the lowest carbon emissions. On March 27, the Obama administration proposed the first-ever rule to limit greenhouse gas emissions from new power plants. Natural gas plants are expected to meet the standard, but coal burners will have a much harder time. "The electricity sector is the principal growth area for natural gas under carbon dioxide emission constraints," said an M.I.T. study titled "The Future of Natural Gas."

Another advantage, according to Richard McMahon, a vice president of finance and energy supply at the Edison Electric Institute, is that natural gas plants are cheaper to build than coal plants.

MICHAEL F. MCELROY FOR THE NEW YORK TIMES

There are about 1,000 natural gas stations in the United States (compared with nearly 160,000 gasoline stations) and only half of those are open to the public.

"Natural gas generally has a smaller footprint," he said. "Coal plants need to store coal, but natural gas plants get their fuel from a pipeline and don't need physical storage." The Obama greenhouse rules would widen the price gap by requiring new coal plants to include carbon capture technology.

The United States still has a big investment in coal plants, and a transition will be gradual. The federal Energy Information Administration estimates that electricity generation from natural gas will increase about 9 percent in 2012, at the same time that coal production declines almost 5 percent. If there is a constraint on utility commitment to natural gas, it is the fuel's history of large price fluctuations.

Thomas Farrell, chairman and chief executive of Dominion Resources, a utility that delivers electric power and natural gas to four states, describes natural gas as "very volatile in its pricing. We're a utility whose customers rely on us to think through 60-year power plant investments, and we've found that the best approach is to have diverse sources and not depend on one predominant source of fuel."

But he added that the company was definitely benefiting from low natural gas prices now. Dominion Virginia Power's 13 percent natural gas electricity production in 2010 jumped to 17 percent in 2011. The company recently completed a natural gas plant and is constructing another, but it also has large nuclear and coal investments.

The share of natural gas as a transportation fuel has never been large, but it is growing rapidly. Refueling is an issue, because there are about 1,000 natural gas stations in the United States (compared with nearly 160,000 gasoline stations) and only half of those are open to the public. Only one automaker, Honda, sells a natural gas passenger car on the American market, and consumers are unlikely to buy them in large numbers any time soon. But the opportunities for truck fleets are quite different.

Almost 40 percent of new garbage trucks and 25 percent of new transit buses can run on natural gas, said the trade organization Natural Gas Vehicles for America. Dan Ustian, chief executive of the truck maker Navistar, said that garbage truck number could grow to 50 percent by the end of next year. Navistar is also building long-range trucks.

Although natural gas cars and small trucks usually run on compressed natural gas, known as C.N.G., to avoid frequent refueling, the larger trucks will mostly use the liquefied form, L.N.G., which has much greater energy density per volume (but must be kept at very cold "cryogenic" temperatures).

Mr. Ustian estimates that, because of quick paybacks with a $1.50 a gallon equivalent price advantage, natural gas could capture 10 percent to 20 percent of the new tractor-trailer vehicle market within a year.

Chrysler, Ford and General Motors have all recently introduced "bifuel" pickup trucks that can run on both natural gas and gasoline. To ensure that such trucks have a place to fill up, Navistar has joined with a natural gas provider, Clean Energy Fuels, and Pilot-Flying J Travel Centers to locate stations 250 miles apart along Interstates. By the end of the year, Clean Energy hopes to have 75 stations open in 33 states.

Andrew Littlefair, president and chief executive of Clean Energy, said that the aim was to make natural gas refueling available on the major trucking corridors. “You don’t need 23,000 truck stops with natural gas,” he said. “You need hundreds in the right places and you can move a lot of fuel. These stations will be where the trucks go now, and the economics look very good.”

In March, Chesapeake Energy, a major natural gas producer, and General Electric said they would collaborate on developing natural gas infrastructure for vehicles, including construction of more than 250 C.N.G. stations beginning this fall.

The prospects exist for American producers to become significant natural gas exporters. In 2011, Dominion won approval from the Energy Department to export L.N.G. from its Cove Point terminal in the Chesapeake Bay to about 20 countries that have free trade agreements with the United States. It has applied for a permit to service the rest of the world. Dominion said that its terminal work force — initially intended to handle imports before the United States became a powerhouse producer — could nearly double with the added workload.

“It’s definitely ironic,” Mr. Farrell said. “Ten years ago, even the futurists wouldn’t have predicted that we’d be exporting natural gas today.”

CHAPTER 4

The Decline of Coal

From the most prolific energy source in early industrial America to a new modern reality: Mining and consuming coal produces an enormous amount of pollution, and it is less efficient than alternatives like nuclear energy and oil. In the late 20th and early 21st centuries, when environmental protection became more urgent, demand for coal experienced a sharp decline. This decline had a political impact: Donald Trump made coal a signature campaign issue and persuaded voters in coal country to support his bid for the presidency. President Trump's victory has not ultimately helped the coal industry, and some of the economic and social fallout is documented in these articles.

Even in Coal Country, the Fight for an Industry

BY ERIC LIPTON | MAY 29, 2012

LOUISA, KY. — For generations, coal has been king in this Appalachian town. It provided heat, light and jobs for the hundreds of people who worked in the nearby coal mines and the smoke-coughing Big Sandy power plant that burned their black bounty.

But now, coal is in a corner. Across the United States, the industry is under siege, threatened by new regulations from Washington, environmentalists fortified by money from Michael R. Bloomberg, the billionaire mayor of New York City, and natural gas companies intent on capturing much of the nation's energy market.

So when the operator of the Big Sandy plant announced last year

SHAWN POYNTER FOR THE NEW YORK TIMES

A coal wall at a Kentucky mine. The use of coal is declining because of new pollution rules and a surge in natural gas production.

that it would be switching from coal to cleaner, cheaper natural gas, people here took it as the worst betrayal imaginable.

"Have you lost your mind?" State Representative Rocky Adkins, a Democrat and one of Kentucky's most powerful politicians, thundered at Michael G. Morris, the chairman of the plant's operator, American Electric Power, during an encounter last summer. "You cannot wave the white flag and let the environmentalists and regulators declare victory here in the heart of coal country."

Coal and electric utilities, long allied, are beginning to split. More than 100 of the 500 or so coal-burning power plants in the United States are expected to be shut down in the next few years. While coal still provides about a third of the nation's power, just four years ago it was providing nearly half.

The decline is largely because new pollution rules have made coal plants more costly, while a surge in production of natural gas through the process of hydraulic fracturing, known as fracking, has sent gas prices plummeting. Together, the economics of coal have been transformed after a century of dominance in Washington, state capitals and the board rooms of electric utilities.

"The math screams at you to do gas," said Mr. Morris, whose company is the nation's largest consumer of coal.

Environmental groups, after years of targeting coal plants as leading sources of air pollution, have moved in for the kill. "We never thought we would get to a place where coal plants are falling so fast," said Bruce Nilles, the director of the Sierra Club's Beyond Coal initiative. It has been aided by $50 million from Mr. Bloomberg, who views the campaign as part of a public health effort, and $26 million from an odd bedfellow: the top official of a natural gas company.

The environmentalists figure that if they can shut down a third of the nation's coal burning plants by 2020, emissions of greenhouse gases in the United States could be cut at least as much as they would have under a landmark 2009 climate bill that died in Congress.

But the coal industry is mustering all the weapons it can: lobbying, legislation, litigation and a multimillion-dollar advertising campaign trumpeting the benefits of "clean coal." The fight has even become an issue in the presidential campaign, with the industry blaming President Obama and the Environmental Protection Agency for the onslaught, and Mitt Romney, the presumptive Republican nominee, hinting that he would roll back some of the rules.

Here in Kentucky, the intervention by Mr. Adkins and other coal industry advocates has saved coal at Big Sandy, at least temporarily. American Electric Power, which is based in Columbus, Ohio, is proposing a $1 billion retrofit to allow the plant to continue burning coal and has asked Kentucky regulators to approve a 30 percent increase in electricity rates to pay for the work.

But that request, which will come up for a vote by the state's utility commission within the next week, has inspired resistance from some residents, large industrial companies that consume much of Kentucky's electricity and even the state attorney general's office.

Pressured on the domestic front, some giant American coal producers, like Arch Coal and Peabody Energy, are shifting their attention to markets overseas, where coal-fired power plants are being built faster than they are being abandoned in the United States.

Even if Big Sandy continues to eat up 90 rail cars of coal a day, the industry's decline is evident here. Sales to Midwestern power plants have slumped, as has the market price of coal, dropping so suddenly that many local mines are cutting back hours or closing. A warm winter, decreasing demand, only made matters worse.

"I call it the imperfect storm," Mr. Adkins said. "And it is breaking the back of our local economy."

A COORDINATED EFFORT

The anger toward Washington is palpable in this impoverished corner of Eastern Kentucky, where miners display bumper stickers or license plates on their pickup trucks with slogans like "Coal Keeps the Lights On" or "If Obama Is the Answer, How Stupid Was the Question?"

It is hard to find anyone here who does not feel affected by the fate of Big Sandy. Just as the smokestack at the plant towers over the countryside, Big Sandy dominates much of life here.

Danny Sartin, 61, a barrel-chested heavy equipment operator at the plant, said his father, grandfathers and uncles all worked in local mines that feed Big Sandy. "Coal and the coal mining industry, it's all we have ever known," Mr. Sartin said.

Some of that coal comes from the Licking River mine, about 50 miles south of Big Sandy, where miners rip apart hillsides to reach vast seams just below the surface.

Chris Lacy, 41, an executive at Licking River Resources Inc., said layoffs among his 350 miners — in Magoffin County, where unemployment is already 17.5 percent — are inevitable if the coal furnaces at Big Sandy go cold. Even the garden supply company that Mr. Lacy's

SHAWN POYNTER FOR THE NEW YORK TIMES

The Big Sandy power plant near Louisa, Ky. The operator had announced plans to switch from coal to natural gas, prompting an uproar in the area.

father-in-law owns and where his two sons work indirectly relies on Big Sandy, because mines are required to plant grass over the scarred earth they leave behind. "It is the ripple effect that comes right through us," Mr. Lacy said.

Channeling the animosity toward Washington and fears about their livelihoods, coal producers, union leaders, landowners and railroads came together to pressure American Electric Power to back down on its plan to close the coal furnaces at Big Sandy. They have leaned on county judges, state legislators and other politicians to attempt to silence public criticism of the 30 percent electricity rate increase and to pressure the Kentucky Public Service Commission to approve the retrofit project.

Saving coal, they argued, justified the rate increase, which would cost the average residential customer about $472 a year in addition to the typical $1,580 annual bill today.

"I will grant you it is going to cost a lot of money to retrofit that plant," said Nick Carter, the president of a company that represents landowners whose properties hold billions of tons of coal reserves. "But how many teachers will be laid off and how many churches will have to close if Big Sandy stops burning coal?"

At Dee's Drive Inn Restaurant, a fixture on Main Street in Louisa, the patrons are split.

Fred Klinebriel, 58, a disabled former steelworker, said his father was a mine worker and his brother a trucker who moved coal. But if keeping coal means an even bigger electric bill, he is not sure it is worth it. "I am up against the wall right now as it is," he said. "I guess you are damned if you do and damned if you don't — or at least we are here in coal country."

ENVIRONMENTAL ISSUES

What went largely unspoken in the dozens of pages of e-mails, letters and other pitches these players have churned out in the fight to keep the plant open were the perils of coal, which extend far beyond mine accidents and black lung disease.

The Big Sandy plant spews tens of thousands of tons of pollutants each year into the region's air, including sulfur dioxide and smaller amounts of mercury, which can cause health problems like respiratory illnesses and possibly developmental disabilities among children. Many of these pollutants would be significantly reduced with the retrofit, but the plant would continue to be a major source of carbon dioxide, which is blamed for global warming.

Big Sandy also maintains a sprawling coal ash pit near the plant, created to store waste ash after the coal is burned, that the E.P.A. recently listed as one of 45 "high hazard" pits nationwide. That means it "will probably cause loss of human life," the E.P.A. says, if a serious accident occurs. In Tennessee in 2008, a billion gallons of slurry from a coal ash pit washed out area homes and streams, though no deaths resulted.

Meanwhile, federal regulators have accused the owners of Licking River of dumping debris, known as spoil, from another nearby mine into a local valley, harming wildlife and an intermittent local stream.

Mr. Lacy, the Licking River executive, says such concerns are overblown. Instead, he talks of a conspiracy by environmentalists and the Obama administration to destroy the way of life here in Kentucky.

"I at least have to give them some credit," he said. "It has been well played on their part, very methodical, step by step."

Some of the regulations the industry finds objectionable, though, had their origins in a Republican administration. In 1990, President George Bush proposed and Congress approved sweeping revisions to the Clean Air Act, authorizing the E.P.A. to regulate emissions of mercury, arsenic and other toxic airborne chemicals. The agency determined in 2000 that it had the power to limit such emissions from power plants, but a weak rule issued under the second Bush administration was successfully challenged in court by environmental advocates.

The Obama administration, acting under court order, issued new standards in December that would require more emissions reductions by all but the top-performing plants. Gina McCarthy, the director of the Office of Air and Radiation at the E.P.A., said that accusations of collusion between the agency and environmental advocates were unfounded.

"Coal will continue to be a large part of electric generation in this country for a long time," Ms. McCarthy said in an interview. "I just hope it is cleaner."

Mr. Lacy is hardly convinced. As he drove through the Licking River mine during a shift change one recent afternoon, his face reddened.

"If they keep this up, the people who live here are going to have to move somewhere else, like during the Depression," he said. "This place is suffering in a bad way."

SHAWN POYNTER FOR THE NEW YORK TIMES

Chris Lacy, a mining executive, said layoffs among his 350 miners would be inevitable if the coal furnaces at Big Sandy went cold.

UNLIKELY ALLIES

Tacked up on the wall in a cramped office in Columbus, Ohio, that serves as the Midwest headquarters for the Sierra Club is a map of the United States with the headline "Coal Plants Under Target." Dozens of color-coded pins form a giant U shape — from Minnesota, south to Missouri, east to Kentucky and then up to Ohio — with each marking a plant that the Sierra Club is determined to shut down.

For years, the group filed lawsuits to try to force utilities or federal regulators to comply with pollution-control laws and organized public opinion campaigns to try to block the construction of plants. But the change in the energy marketplace has given the environmentalists an extraordinary new weapon: the pocketbooks of consumers.

"The coal industry used to be able to get away with murder, here in Ohio and throughout Appalachia," said Nachy Kanfer, 27, a Sierra Club organizer. "Not anymore."

In late April, Mr. Kanfer and other Sierra Club staff members traveled to Kentucky to testify before the Kentucky Public Service Commission. They argued that American Electric Power should not be allowed to retrofit Big Sandy — an argument they are making in many states — because there are less expensive alternatives to deliver power.

Elsewhere, the Sierra Club and other environmental groups are also pressing local officials in metropolitan areas to help shut down coal-burning power plants. In Chicago, for example, Mayor Rahm Emanuel recently announced that the city's last two coal-fired plants would close in 2014, four years earlier than expected.

One of the most important early allies in this fight was Aubrey K. McClendon, the chief executive of Chesapeake Energy, who donated $26 million starting in 2007 to help the Sierra Club with its campaign.

The company also donated millions of dollars more to the American Lung Association, which used the money, in part, to run "Fighting for Air" television commercials. Some of the most recent ads in the campaign feature a baby coughing, wheezing and then crying while sitting outside a coal-fired power plant.

The Sierra Club came under attack from other environmental activists for accepting money from Mr. McClendon, whose company has a financial interest in killing off its competition but burns a fossil fuel itself. Mr. Nilles, the director of Beyond Coal, now views it as a mistake. "We would not do it again," he said.

Other deep-pocketed donors have stepped in, including Mr. Bloomberg, whose intervention has infuriated Kentucky officials like Mr. Adkins, the legislator.

"Mayor Bloomberg should stay in that high-rise condo or his mansions," Mr. Adkins said, "and eat his caviar while we keep his lights on in New York City."

Big Coal has hardly conceded defeat in this multifront war.

The industry has increased political campaign contributions in the last four years to historic levels, with 80 percent of those donations going to Republicans, according to the Center for Responsive Politics. Companies like Arch Coal, which used to spend only about $100,000 a year on lobbyists in Washington, invested $5.7 million to push its case during the first three years of the Obama administration.

And even as American Electric Power plans to close 5 of its 21 coal-burning plants and rely much more on natural gas, it still intends to retrofit 12 plants. That means it will be burning coal for years to come. A rise in natural gas prices could also slow the decline of coal as a power source. So the company has joined with old allies in Washington to try to delay the new rules and block any future ones.

The industry and its supporters have also gone to court, filing lawsuits challenging E.P.A. rules that limit pollution from coal-burning plants from crossing state lines and the mountaintop mining rules that are holding up new permits in Kentucky and West Virginia — legal fights that the industry has had some success with so far.

But the regional agency that coordinates electric power delivery in the mid-Atlantic and the Midwest cannot wait for the battles to be resolved. This month, it auctioned off the rights for utility companies to supply electricity that will be needed to make up for what is lost through coal plant retirements. Most of the new power is fueled by natural gas.

"It's an unprecedented transition," said Michael J. Kormos, senior vice president for operations at PJM Interconnection, the regional group that coordinates power delivery for 60 million people in 13 states. "But whatever happens, we have to make sure we keep the lights on."

A Bleak Outlook for Trump's Promises to Coal Miners

BY CLIFFORD KRAUSS AND MICHAEL CORKERY | NOV. 19, 2016

DONALD J. TRUMP made coal a centerpiece of his campaign, holding rousing rallies with miners in hard hats, who he said had been neglected under eight years of the Obama administration. The strategy paid off, helping him score crucial wins in Pennsylvania and Ohio.

Now, though, coal may prove a different sort of symbol — that is, of the challenges that the president-elect will face delivering on his many promises to restore struggling sectors of the American economy.

The United States coal industry and the jobs that support it have been in decline for decades as a result of environmental concerns, automation in mining and slowdowns in manufacturing industries that burned coal for power.

And these days, no matter who is president, coal is at the mercy of market economics. Coal's No. 1 rival is cheap, cleaner-burning natural gas — which could become an even more potent competitor under the incoming administration. The probable easing of restrictions on pipeline building and loosening of rules on gas exploration and production would mean more natural gas reaching the market.

Despite recent increases, coal's price has been drifting downward for years. But the price of natural gas has fallen even more sharply.

"I don't think the Trump presidency will have a material impact on bringing coal miners back to work," said Ted O'Brien, a coal analyst at Doyle Trading Consultants, a leading energy industry research firm.

"He may eliminate the regulatory overhang," Mr. O'Brien said, referring to the environmental rules that have cast a shadow over coal, "but I have a hard time seeing a surge in coal demand."

Coal's long decline predates President Obama's arrival in the White House in 2009. The collapse of the American steel industry in late 20th

GEORGE ETHEREDGE FOR THE NEW YORK TIMES

A plant in Buchanan County, Va., where coal mining is a major source of jobs. Donald J. Trump won over 75 percent of the votes in the county.

century reduced demand for the metallurgical coal that is mined most prominently in Appalachia.

In addition, utilities have been slow to build new coal-fired power plants in recent decades because of air-quality concerns over the burning of the other type of coal — thermal coal — that is used for power plants and is mined across the country.

Mr. Trump campaigned to help both kinds of coal recover.

But natural gas may prove unbeatable. The hydraulic fracturing boom in shale fields that began a decade ago flooded the market with cheap natural gas that continues to erode coal's market share. As recently as early 2008, coal was the source of roughly half of the electricity generated in the United States. Now it is down to about 30 percent.

"There's just a lot of gas in this country, and that is going to hold gas prices down," said Scott Sheffield, chief executive of Pioneer

Natural Resources, a major oil and natural gas producer, who said he voted for Mr. Trump.

The bleak outlook for coal may explain why some of the industry's executives have been reluctant to comment on how the Trump presidency may help their business: They may be wary of raising false hopes among their workers. And many may be reluctant to repeat past industry arguments that climate change was a hoax. Instead, coal producers would rather have tax incentives to support environmental improvements for coal-fired plants, as a way to ensure coal's long-term viability even beyond a Trump administration.

"Any exuberance has to be tempered," said Richard Reavey, vice president for government and public affairs at Cloud Peak Energy, a major Western coal producer. "The view should be cautious optimism."

Beyond the declining demand for coal, there has been an even more fundamental factor behind the shift in coal mining employment, which peaked decades ago. As with those in many industries, jobs in mining have fallen victim to automation. High-tech shears can now shave coal from underground seams — work that formerly required hundreds of miners. Surface mining, which has been increasing in recent years, has also replaced many workers with heavy machinery.

As a result, there are now just over 50,000 jobs in the American coal mining industry, down from a peak of more than 250,000 in 1980.

Most of the losses have come in Appalachian mines — which produce coal for making steel and electricity — because they are older, deeper and more expensive to operate. But automation is hitting employment in mines across the country.

"The industry is simply not going to produce the number of jobs that were historically available in the coal fields," said Patrick C. McGinley, a law professor at West Virginia University, who focuses on coal issues.

A few years ago coal executives hoped exports — which represent about 8 percent of national production — would boom along

Coal's Long Fall

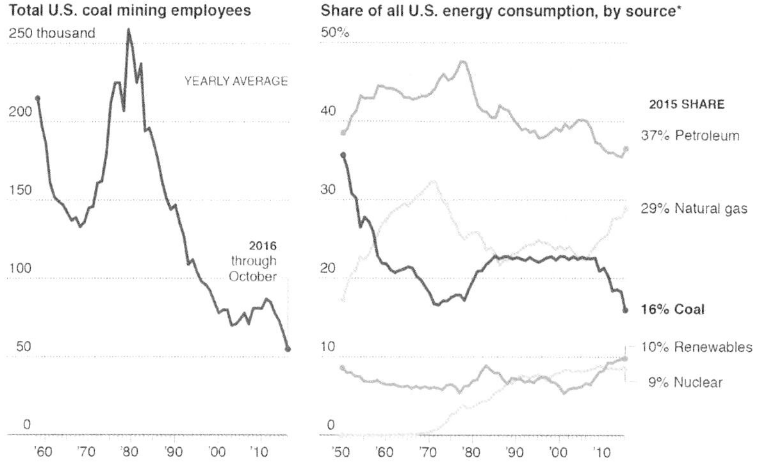

*Note: Consumption includes residential, commercial, transportation and electricity. 2015 shares do not add to 100 due to rounding.

THE NEW YORK TIMES

Coal mining employment began falling from its peak in the early 1980s, as industry practices like mountaintop removal meant fewer workers were needed. Coal's share of total energy consumption is now less than half what it was in the 1950s.

with the economies of China and the developing world. But exports peaked in 2012.

Since then, slower economic growth in the developing world, along with climate and pollution concerns, have depressed demand for coal.

The same considerations have prompted international development banks and large investment companies like JPMorgan Chase and Bank of America to pull back on financing new coal-fired plants — a trend that is unlikely to change under Mr. Trump.

The Trump administration could help the coal industry somewhat by unwinding President Obama's Clean Power Plan, which was designed to replace coal-fired utility plants with those using natural gas and renewable energy sources. But the effects of the plan so far may be hard to reverse.

The tighter air pollution regulations, which are still under challenge in court, forced utilities to choose between revamping aging coal-fired power plants to make them cleaner, or switching to natural gas or green sources like wind and solar. Utilities across the country typically decided to switch.

Last year, as a result, 94 coal-fired power plants were closed across the country, and this year 40 more are expected to close by the end of December. It is most unlikely that Mr. Trump could do anything to bring those plants back online.

"All the older power plants that burned Eastern coal have been basically torn down, dismantled, put in mothballs, some of them permanently," said Robert J. Zik, the now-retired former vice president for operations at TECO Coal, a subsidiary of TECO Energy that was sold to another operator last year.

Other marginal measures the Trump administration might be able to take on coal's behalf, industry executives say, include rolling back the rules that protect streams from surface mining and easing those for leases and royalties on coal mined on federal lands.

Industry executives say that to extend the life of at least some of the 400 or so coal-burning power plants still in use in the United States, the Trump administration and lawmakers in Congress could work with them on "clean coal" initiatives.

Acknowledging that climate change is an issue even if Mr. Trump does not, Mr. Reavey of Cloud Peak Energy wants federal incentives for utilities to refit existing power plants to burn coal more efficiently and to attach systems to their facilities that will capture carbon emissions and sink them permanently in the ground. Such systems, known as carbon capture and sequestration, are currently so costly that utilities simply prefer to replace coal-fired plants with gas-fired ones.

Even before Mr. Trump's election, prices of some types of American coal — particularly the metallurgical variety that is mostly mined in Appalachia and is used to make steel — had been rallying.

That, in turn, had sent the stock prices of some coal mining operations soaring in recent months — a huge win for hedge funds that bought up the debt and equity of the companies when they were cheap.

But the big driver for coal's price run-up was the dwindling supply, as American producers cut back even as Chinese mines were curbing their own production in recent months. Those price benefits are expected to be short-lived, as demand is depressed both by China's pivot toward cleaner fuels to address the country's endemic air pollution and by its new focus on a less energy-intensive consumer economy.

"There is optimism that with government support, coal is more viable," said Mr. O'Brien, the industry analyst. "But the same headwinds still exist that have existed over the past five years."

Coal Museum Sees the Future; Trump Doesn't

OPINION | BY THOMAS L. FRIEDMAN | APRIL 19, 2017

DID YOU CATCH this gem on CNN.com from April 6? "The Kentucky Coal Mining Museum in Benham, owned by Southeast Kentucky Community and Technical College, is switching to solar power to save money. ... Communications director Brandon Robinson told CNN affiliate WYMT that the project 'will help save at least eight to ten thousand dollars, off the energy costs on this building alone.' "

Go figure. The coal mining museum is going solar, for solid economic reasons, and President Trump is reviving coal, with no economic logic at all. This bizarre contrast speaks to a deeper question of leadership and how we judge presidents.

Trump took two major national security decisions in the past few weeks. One was to strike Syria for using poison gas. Trump summoned his national security team, asked for options on Syria, chose the cruise-missile strike — which was right — and won praise for acting "presidential."

The other decision you didn't see. It was Trump dismantling budgets and regulations undergirding U.S. climate and environmental protection policies — in his nutty effort to revive U.S. coal-fired energy — while quietly announcing plans to withhold a promised $32.5 million U.S. contribution for the U.N. Population Fund, which supports family planning and maternal health.

Unlike the Syria decision, Trump made the second move without seeking a comprehensive briefing from experts — he controls the world's greatest collection of climate scientists at NASA, NOAA, the E.P.A., the Pentagon and the C.I.A. — and without ever asking for an intelligence briefing on how the combination of climate change, environmental degradation, drought and population explosions helped trigger the civil war in Syria, spawn terrorist groups like Boko Haram

GEORGE ETHEREDGE FOR THE NEW YORK TIMES

A statue of a coal miner in Benham, Ky.

around Africa's central Lake Chad (which has lost 90 percent of its water mass since 1963) and become the main force pushing tens of thousands of migrants from sub-Saharan Africa into Europe each year, and from Central America up to the U.S.

I promise you that Trump will spend the rest of his presidency dealing with the disruptions caused by this cocktail of population explosion and climate/environmental degradation — and his generals know it. But in today's politics, bombing is considered presidential and ignoring science and defunding family planning, when populations are exploding and droughts expanding, are ho-hum back-page news.

Since Trump seems to be pivoting from some of his campaign nonsense, one can only hope he will do the same on these issues. If Trump is looking for a blueprint, he could not do better than to read a smart new book, "Climate of Hope," by a most unlikely duo: former Sierra Club executive director Carl Pope and billionaire and former New York City Mayor Michael Bloomberg.

When Carl met Mike … It was 2011, Pope went to Bloomberg with a plan for generating bottom-up community activism to help shut down as many coal-fired power plants in America as possible, so another generation of American kids wouldn't be afflicted with childhood asthma and another generation of coal workers wouldn't have to make a living breathing coal dust.

Bloomberg put $50 million into the effort, and the rest is — helping to make coal — history, thanks to the Sierra Club mobilizing communities and technology making natural gas (when the methane leakage is controlled) a much cleaner, cheaper base-load power source for utilities, and wind and solar energy so much more cost-effective.

When the Sierra Club and Bloomberg started in 2011, there were 514 coal-fired power plants in America; since then, 254 have announced they will shut down. They expect that fully two-thirds will be phased out by 2022 — no matter what Trump says or does.

"Climate of Hope" is about how to build on this, by reframing the interrelated challenges of climate change, clean air, clean water and population "from questions of who is going to sacrifice to who is going to grab the profits," Bloomberg explained in an interview. Each of these challenges, he said, can be met in ways that enable cities and countries to make themselves more prosperous, innovative, healthy and secure — if we just get the incentives right.

Imagine, added Pope, that every U.S. company joined Anheuser-Busch in committing to getting all of its electricity from renewable sources. Imagine that instead of subsidizing surplus cotton, destroying the livelihoods of small farmers in Africa, the U.S. government subsidized our farmers to grow crops that restore carbon and store water in their soils, thus drought-proofing Texas and California.

Imagine every U.S. city joining those already buying electric self-driving vehicles, thereby scaling a new auto-on-demand industry — while reducing the need for personal cars and the parking places and garages for them — thereby unlocking so much real estate for growth and easing urban housing prices. Imagine that instead of vowing to bring back coal mining jobs, our president offered to link West Virginia and the nation's most prosperous metropolitan economy, Washington, D.C., with high-speed rail service.

Imagine ... we could actually make America great again, not just prolong a dying coal industry! Now *that* would be presidential.

THOMAS L. FRIEDMAN is an Op-Ed columnist for The New York Times.

Where Wind Farms Meet Coal Country, There's Enduring Faith in Trump

BY CLIFFORD KRAUSS | DEC. 14, 2017

Hoping for more unfettered production of coal, oil and gas even as it erects wind farms, a Wyoming county sees the President as a key to job security.

GLENROCK, WYO. — No place is more likely than this one to benefit from President Trump's promise to make the United States a dominant energy force in the world, or more likely to be disappointed if the promise is not kept.

A sparsely populated expanse of windswept rolling meadows and sharp bluffs filled with pine trees and the occasional ranch and hay farm, Converse County also has some of the country's richest resources: the nation's third-largest coal mine, its largest uranium production facility, four big wind farms, more than a thousand oil and gas wells, and a large coal-fired power plant.

But diversified in nothing but energy, the county and nearly the entire state of Wyoming are acutely vulnerable to commodity prices. And while oil and coal prices have headed higher of late, they remain far below the levels of recent years, resulting in layoffs and plummeting tax receipts.

"For sale" signs dot nearly every residential neighborhood as young energy workers have left to seek jobs in healthier labor markets in Colorado and Utah. Occupancy at the Higgins Hotel, a landmark in this town of 2,500, dropped 80 percent between 2014 and 2016, and according to Doug Frank, the owner, this year there has been "a slight uptick, but nothing noticeable yet."

Nevertheless, like so many others here, Mr. Frank, who is also mayor of Glenrock, has not lost faith in the president.

DAMON WINTER/THE NEW YORK TIMES

Cameco Resources' Smith Ranch-Highland mine near Glenrock is part of the nation's largest uranium production facility. A worker tested a well into which water and resin are injected to extract uranium.

"The mind-set is huge — it is what is driving the people here," Mayor Frank said while shaking margaritas and his own high-octane concoctions for customers at the Antelope Bar in his hotel. "The most amazing thing about his base is the willingness to forgive the cacophony. We see a greater good coming."

The greater good, in the view of local residents from energy executives to roustabouts, depends on slashing environmental regulations, including restrictions on pipeline building that could deliver more Wyoming oil and gas to faraway markets. They applaud the lifting of the moratorium on coal leasing on federal lands. Many approve of Mr. Trump's rejection of the Paris climate accord, and the administration's move to unwind President Barack Obama's Clean Power Plan, which was designed to control power plant emissions.

They express hope that the president can limit oil imports while encouraging more production and exports. The unflinching sentiment

DAMON WINTER/THE NEW YORK TIMES

Mayor Doug Frank of Glenrock, center, with his wife, Maribel, on a night out in Casper, 25 miles away. "We see a greater good coming," Mr. Frank said of the region's prospects under President Trump.

may best be expressed by a sticker appearing on the back of some local pickup trucks that says "Trump 2017-2025," with the T depicted as a gushing oil well.

"My livelihood, taking care of my family, depended on Trump's election," said Bryant Michael, a 27-year-old technician who fills heavy oil-field equipment and trucks with fuel. Unemployed for a year, he was hired in May as drilling began to pick up again.

"I think Washington is a main factor in where we get our oil and what we do with it," he said. "Somebody was whispering in Obama's ear. Every time there's a Democrat in the White House, there's hardly any work in the oil field."

Actually, oil and gas exploration soared during most of the Obama administration before it swooned in the final two years. But Mr. Trump's embrace of coal mining and unfettered energy production is particularly welcome here, since almost everyone is dependent on energy jobs — coal miners and their families, out-of-state oil workers who drill and complete wells, and the business owners and service workers catering to everyone. This is a place that gauges its well-being by the local rig count and, since big-time coal mining began here in the 1970s and 1980s, how often mile-long coal trains pass by.

Things could still be going far better. During the first nine months of the year, coal production at Cloud Peak Energy's Antelope Mine, a pillar of the local economy, increased by a fraction of 1 percent over the same period in 2016, a particularly weak year. Employment at the mine peaked in 2015 at 616, and is now around 530 — equal to what it was when Mr. Trump was inaugurated — even though the nation's coal exports are up this year.

And there has been little regulatory relief so far, energy executives note. The end of the moratorium on leasing on federal lands means more certainty that the Antelope Mine can be extended someday, but that would not make a difference for more than five years into the future, and only if there is greater demand for coal.

But there are some positive signs. Coal prices have risen, along with natural gas, in part because demand is up in South Korea, Japan and parts of Europe. Four large wind farms have been built in recent years, including one completed last fall, and expansions are on the way. But all of them together, according to county officials, employ at most 100 workers full time.

"People think Trump is a good guy, so people trust his judgment," said Robert G. Short, a leading Glenrock businessman who is vice chairman of the Converse County commissioners. But he added: "Are we going back to where we were? The simple answer is no. Coal is diminished and never will likely come back."

Though few people here say so, the energy workers of Converse County are competing with one another. The hydraulic-fracturing boom is coaxing more natural gas out of the local shale fields, which lowers both gas and coal prices and depresses the attractiveness of nuclear energy. And the growing wind power — helped along by tax incentives enacted at the end of the Obama administration — ultimately eats into the market share of all the other energy sources.

And yet the workers in all the energy sources wistfully see themselves as having common goals and say Mr. Trump may offer the county its last big hope.

A SEARCH FOR SECURITY

The coal-fired Dave Johnston Power Plant, outside Glenrock, is like a monument to the county's energy legacy. Its giant chimneys and plumes of smoke dominate the skyline by day, while at night it offers a display of colors so bright it looks like a small city from the Rocky Mountain foothills nearby. It is where Shawn Gates is living the Wyoming dream, though he knows it may be ending sooner rather than later.

Since going to work in 2011 at the plant, where his father is also employed, he has worked his way up to become a control room operator and makes more than $40 an hour. With overtime and shift differentials, he has, at 36, acquired a solidly middle-class living. He, his wife and their four children live in a comfortable ranch house with a motorboat and a recreational vehicle in the front yard and a trampoline in the back, along with eight horses.

His 10-year-old son, Guthry, hopes to work in the plant as well, extending the family's foothold there to a fourth generation.

During the presidential campaign last year, Mr. Gates said, "job security was on my mind," especially after Hillary Clinton said she was "going to put a lot of coal miners and coal companies out of business." Now he feels better.

"I think my job is fairly secure," he said during a chat at his kitchen table. "I don't think it would have been under Hillary. I can't find another job like mine."

But even as he praises Mr. Trump's goals, he sees warning signs. "I think he will keep fossil fuels operating and keep E.P.A. within limits,"

Mr. Gates said, referring to the Environmental Protection Agency. But knitting his brow with concern, he added, “They’re putting all these wind turbines up that are not cost effective, at the taxpayer’s expense.”

Mr. Gates’s wife, Jesi, a nurse, said Mr. Trump’s election was great for Wyoming, but “he can only do so much as one person.” She noted that the power plant was tentatively scheduled to be shut down in a decade, adding: “That 2027 date definitely looms in your mind. At least my kids will have graduated from high school by then.”

Mr. Gates grew up in Glenrock, and worked for a while as a ranch hand, maintained water wells and did some electrical work. On the side, he took online business classes. But he always had energy on his mind — “that’s what Wyoming is,” he said.

When it was time to raise a family, he followed in his father’s footsteps for the steady salary and insurance. He has done well at the plant, moving from the coal yard to his current position as assistant auxiliary operator responsible for the vital task of checking motors and oil levels.

Like many in Converse County, Mr. Gates expresses a strong distrust for Washington and elites in general. “You need to clean house of politicians,” he said, calling for term limits for Congress.

Even his attitude toward Mr. Trump is not entirely positive: “I think he’s blunt. I don’t think he is dishonest, but I don’t think he’s 100 percent truthful, either.” Still, he said, “he got elected, so let him do his job.”

WIND JOBS, COAL ATTITUDES

Woody Ricker, a 38-year-old technician at Duke Energy’s Top of the World wind farm outside Glenrock, comes at the energy picture from a different perspective. But his views, like those of many wind workers here, are surprisingly similar to those of workers whose jobs rely on coal.

For years, he has been teased by friends for having an “Obama job” in an area where wind farms are seen as taking business from the coal industry. He also knows that the growth of renewable energy sources

DAMON WINTER/THE NEW YORK TIMES

From the Rocky Mountain foothills, the Dave Johnston Power Plant, outside Glenrock, looks like a small city.

in recent years, like the one responsible for his employment, has a lot to do with concerns about climate change.

But Mr. Ricker, like most of his neighbors in and around the town of Douglas, isn't particularly convinced that humans have much impact on climate change.

"I am not convinced on what has caused the change in climate," he said. "Doing a fix without finding a root cause? I don't see it."

He anticipated the next question. "So why am I working in the wind industry?" he asked. "I'm not in it for that. I'm in it to produce more American energy, to make it more stable."

Mr. Ricker, who lives with his wife, Stacey, and their three children in a house surrounded by craggy bluffs and sunflowers, fell into the wind business. Having grown up here and studied biology in college, he owned a local construction company with his father until business dried up during the last recession. When some men who came by to look at one of his properties liked his handiwork, they suggested that he apply for a job with their wind contract business.

Needing good health insurance to pay for his daughter's hip surgery, he made the switch and eventually went to Duke when the big utility took over operations of the wind farm. At a time when many states and business customers are demanding more clean energy, Mr. Ricker is not worried that Mr. Trump might turn against renewables.

"I have had people presume my political leanings because of my job — incorrectly, for the record," he said.

Although Mr. Ricker has no family roots in the energy business — his father was an assistant pastor who was also a cowboy — he relates to fossil fuels as much as he does to wind.

"Coal and oil are what keep the value of my house where it is," he said. "I'm hugely in favor of American energy, and if I'm going to pick a state that it will benefit, it's Wyoming."

A coal man would not have said it much differently.

'I DON'T HAVE TO LIKE HIM'

Slowly but surely, women are entering the energy work force, and while they tend to be as outspoken as the men, their views sometimes sharply differ.

Pam Graham, a truck driver at the Cloud Peak mine, is a rarity in Converse County. She's a Democrat who thinks that climate change is no hoax, that the Affordable Care Act should be fixed and not scrapped, and that as for immigration, "the idea of building a wall is a stupid thing."

Her choicest words are aimed at Mr. Trump's treatment of women, which she describes as disrespectful. "I get tired of the tweeting," she said. "And that whole thing with the grabbing of women, that's just nasty."

"Those women should have decked him," she said sternly as she steered 240 tons of coal loaded on her Komatsu haul truck through the deep canyons of the strip mine. She quickly smiled, and added with a knowing chuckle, "I would have given him a black eye."

DAMON WINTER/THE NEW YORK TIMES

The Dave Johnston Power Plant is tentatively scheduled to be shut down in a decade. "That 2027 date definitely looms in your mind," said Jesi Gates, whose husband works there.

But when she cast her ballot, she said, there was no doubt that she would vote for Mr. Trump.

While not an ideological conservative, Ms. Graham looks to the president to bolster the fortunes of Converse County energy, and in the end that was the most important consideration in choosing him over Mrs. Clinton.

"I don't have to like him as a person," she explained. "I was thinking if she won, in a few years we'd probably be out of work. Am I going to find another job that pays $30 an hour?"

At 53, Ms. Graham is an avid motorcycle rider who brings a personal style to her job. "There's a view of a coal miner with a black face and dirty fingers, and I don't look like one — I dress up," she said. "When I go out to do errands, I like to wear fashionable girlie clothes."

Before she enters her truck cabin for the day's first run, she sprays disinfectant on the seats and thoroughly wipes off the dashboard. "I'm probably a little unconventional, yeah," she said.

Perhaps unsurprisingly, Ms. Graham came to her job in an unconventional way, though her grandfather worked in the oil and gas business as a tool pusher and her stepfather drove water trucks in the oil field. Local coal mining was still in its infancy when she grew up in Douglas, so after dropping out of junior college, she waited on tables and worked as a bartender. She had a child, divorced and worked as a bank teller and personal loan officer for nearly 12 years.

Tired of banking, she saw an advertisement in the newspaper for coal truck drivers, applied and started working for Cloud Peak. She said the toughest thing about learning the job had been her fear of heights, since a truck cabin is as high off the ground as the roof of a house. "I didn't look down from the truck for two years," she said.

Ms. Graham has remarried, to an old high school friend who is a contractor, and she helps take care of five grandchildren. She is one of 61 women employed by the mine. For her, the best thing that Mr. Trump brings is more security.

"Before the election, I felt my livelihood was threatened — not just my job, but my way of life," she said. "We have a house and a mortgage, and there are 130-some houses on the market around Douglas, so where are we going to go?"

She is less than enthusiastic about the president's performance, but said he was, at least, putting a spotlight on coal's importance. "We're the redheaded stepchild," she said. "People don't understand that if it weren't for us, and they turned on the heat, nothing would happen."

ROBERT GEBELOFF contributed reporting from New York.

Coal's Decline Seems Impervious to Trump's Promises

BY CLIFFORD KRAUSS | JAN. 24, 2018

BOBTOWN, PA. — When Nic Zmija applied for a job at the 4 West coal mine three years ago, he was tantalized by a fat raise and a secure future. Once hired, he was told that someday even his two young sons had jobs waiting for them.

"It all sounded good," Mr. Zmija recalled with a tight smile while sitting at his kitchen table the other day. "They said my kids would be able to retire here."

But right after New Year's, management announced that the mine would have to close, leaving 370 workers scrambling to find new jobs. The Zmija family must now prepare to move in search of the next coal job.

The fateful turn of events in Appalachian mining towns like Bobtown, isolated between craggy bluffs and wooded hills 70 miles south of Pittsburgh, illustrates the seemingly relentless downturn of the coal industry. While President Trump has offered some regulatory relief to the industry, market forces still dictate a gloomy future — one largely shaped by the glut of cheap natural gas yielded by the drilling boom in shale fields near here and across much of the nation.

As aging coal-fired power plants are shut — roughly 20 of 380 have closed or are in the process of shutting since Mr. Trump took office — coal's share of the nation's power mix has plummeted from nearly half in 2008 to roughly a third today.

Last year, coal consumption in the United States fell by 2.4 percent, falling to its lowest level in nearly four decades. In the early weeks of 2018, national coal production has continued to decline from a year ago despite the frigid winter. A weather-related increase in exports last year yielded a modest gain in jobs, but it is not considered sustainable.

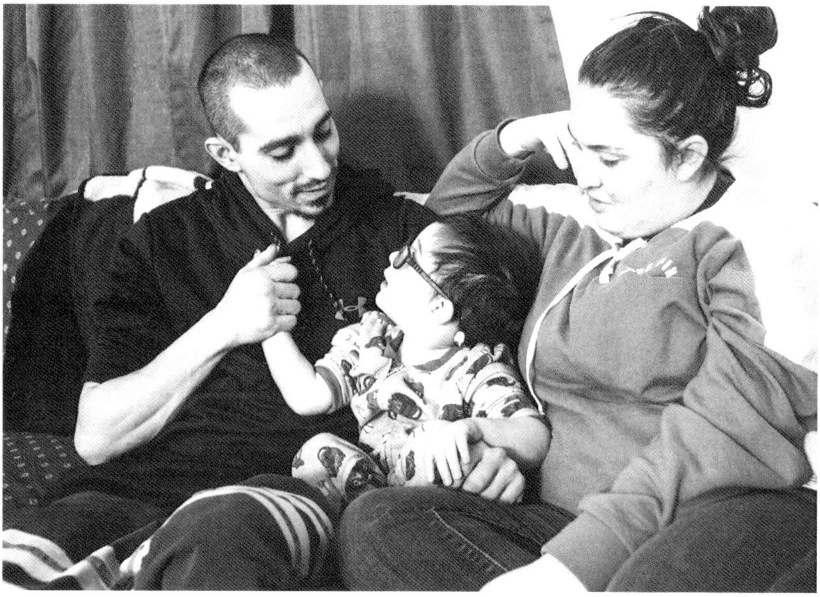

ANDREW SPEAR FOR THE NEW YORK TIMES

Nic Zmija with his son, Kolson, and wife, Beth, at their home in Bobtown, Pa. Mr. Zmija moved his family from Maryland for a better-paying mining job at 4 West, which is closing.

The decline in demand has forced a 38 percent drop in the nation's coal production in a little less than a decade. Now only the most efficient mines containing the highest-quality coal are able to survive.

The 4 West mine, like many that produce coal for power utilities in Appalachia, is expensive to run. Its coal seam is thin and of lower quality than competing mines, and its traditional form of mining requires costly methods to stabilize roofs to protect against the kind of accidents that caused the deaths of two miners at 4 West over the last three years. Government fines and management turmoil also took their toll.

The most successful mines these days, particularly here in Appalachia, produce metallurgical coal for steel making in the United States and abroad. 4 West produces only thermal coal for a nearby power plant, which will now rely on other local mines.

ANDREW SPEAR FOR THE NEW YORK TIMES

The Longview Power Plant in West Virginia, which the 4 West mine in nearby Greene County, Pa., has supplied with thermal coal. The most successful Appalachian mines these days produce higher-quality coal for steel making.

"It's just come to a point where the mine is not economical to continue," said Brian Osborn, senior vice president for operations for Mepco Holdings, owner of the 4 West mine.

The stress is being particularly felt here in Greene County, where coal mines have been closing for years, chewing-tobacco advertisements adorn the sides of barns, and graffiti claiming that the Environmental Protection Agency has "ruined this country" defaces the road sign at the entrance of one abandoned mine.

Three coal mines are left here, after one closed nearly two years ago, laying off roughly 500 workers as its owner, Alpha Natural Resources, curtailed its operations while filing for bankruptcy protection. A total of 2,000 coal miners work in the county, but that number will be shaved by nearly 20 percent by June 1 after workers finish cleaning up the 4 West mine and remove equipment for the final closing.

ANDREW SPEAR FOR THE NEW YORK TIMES

The conveyor belt at 4 West mine, owned by Mepco Holdings, where 370 workers will lose their jobs. Domestic demand continues to fall as coal is displaced by natural gas in power plants.

Blair Zimmerman, the chairman of the Greene County Board of Commissioners, estimated that the county's unemployment rate, currently 5.2 percent, will jump by 1.5 percentage points.

"It's a major impact — it's tax revenue, it's jobs, it's the housing market," said Mr. Zimmerman, a former coal mine worker and a Democrat. "If they can't make the wages here, they'll move away."

Painful adjustments have already begun. Most of the miners said they would look for other mining jobs, and their company is giving them days off to go to interviews.

William Laviolette, a 26-year-old maintenance worker at the mine who made roughly $55,000 last year, said that if he didn't find another mine job, he would go back to school to get his high school degree.

He said he had cut his daily two-pack cigarette habit to one to save money. His wife, Ashley, has taken part-time work as a custodian at a furniture store, and the family has canceled a vacation to

Walt Disney World. He has even stopped buying wood to make toys for his two children.

"We just buy the essentials now, toilet paper and food," Mr. Laviolette said. "I was told we have at least 175 to 200 years of coal. Now I have to keep my eyes out for other jobs."

Business has already dried up at bars and restaurants where the miners used to eat, shoot pool and joke around after work. "This is going to kill this community," said Debbie Bauza, a server at Huddle House, a favorite breakfast spot for workers getting off the overnight shift.

Mr. Trump won 68 percent of the county's vote — 10 percentage points more than Mitt Romney four years before — with his promises to revive the coal industry. Most of the miners say they continue to support him despite their turn in fortunes.

"He's trying his best," said Rick Glover, a 4 West mine conveyor-belt attendant. "You can't change the country overnight."

Since taking office a year ago, Mr. Trump has renounced the Paris climate change agreement and sought to loosen a variety of regulations on mining and power plants. Some efforts have been delayed in court, and a recent administration effort to subsidize nuclear and coal-fired plants was shot down by regulators.

Nevertheless, coal executives say the issuing of federal permits for mining operations has become more certain and quicker.

"I would definitely say the Trump administration has benefited the industry," said Rachel Gleason, executive director of the Pennsylvania Coal Alliance. "I don't know if there are that many new policies, but many of the policies that were threatening the industry are no longer in play."

Nationwide, there was a 1 percent increase in coal mining jobs last year, to just over 50,000, mostly because of an increase in mining metallurgical coal for export to Asia. There was a net increase of roughly 100 jobs in Pennsylvania, largely related to the opening of three new metallurgical coal mines.

ANDREW SPEAR FOR THE NEW YORK TIMES

William Laviolette, who works at 4 West, and his wife, Ashley, who picked up part-time custodial work to help make ends meet.

Coal prices in Asia soared after a cyclone knocked out production in Australia early last year, producing an opening for American exports.

"I don't think that President Trump, when he promised to bring about a recovery in U.S. coal mining, intended to do it by way of boosting Chinese steel production," said Trevor Houser, a coal expert at Rhodium Group, an economic analysis firm. "That is what is driving the recovery."

Energy experts say that coal exports should plateau this year, and that domestic consumption of thermal coal for electricity should continue its long decline.

Even many coal-producing states are switching to natural gas for power, in part because, like Pennsylvania, they produce increasing amounts of shale gas. The power-fuel mix supplying the PJM regional transmission electrical grid, which serves 13 states including Pennsylvania, West Virginia and Kentucky, went from 55 percent coal and 8 percent natural gas in 2006 to 34 percent coal and 27 percent gas last year.

The Energy Department projected this month that the price of natural gas would decline this year because of increased production and pipeline completions, and that its share of electricity generation would increase nationwide to 34 percent by 2019, from 32 percent.

Over the same period, coal is to decline to 28 percent from 30 percent. Renewable sources not including hydroelectric power, which currently account for 10 percent of energy supplies, are expected to climb to 11 percent.

At age 28, Mr. Zmija, like most of the coal mineworkers here, has not lost faith in the industry. He is considering applying for a coal job in Alabama, or he may return to his old mine job in Maryland, although it pays far less than the $106,000 he made last year at 4 West. A sign in his living room says, "I'm a proud coal miner."

Still, he grumbles about the turn of fortune at 4 West, saying, "It feels like a slap in the face."

Trump's New Pollution Rules Still Won't Save the Coal Industry

BY BRAD PLUMER | AUG. 22, 2018

WASHINGTON — America's ailing coal industry was buoyed on Tuesday when the Environmental Protection Agency unveiled a proposal to relax pollution regulations on coal-fired power plants. President Trump traveled to West Virginia to tout the planned measure, telling supporters, "We're putting our great coal miners back to work."

Yet the reality on the ground for the nation's coal industry remains bleak. Even the Trump administration's own numbers suggest that its latest proposal won't reverse the sharp decline of coal power, which has been crushed by competition from cheaper natural gas and renewable energy over the past decade.

More than 200 coal plants have shut down since 2010, and another 40 plants have announced they will close in the years ahead, with virtually no new coal plants being built today.

At best, if finalized, the E.P.A.'s newest rollback could help a small number of those endangered coal plants stave off retirement for a bit longer, albeit at the expense of increased air pollution. But even in that scenario, the agency's own analysis showed, coal power would still decline by 20 percent between now and 2030 and coal mining would drop by one-third.

The E.P.A. said the new rules could lead to as many as 1,400 more deaths a year.

"This is like throwing a few snowballs into a blizzard," said Tom Sanzillo, director of finance at the Institute for Energy Economics and Financial Analysis. "You might see a plant here or a plant there that benefits from the new rules. But we're talking about very minor changes compared with the significant gap between the cost of coal and the cost of natural gas."

GABRIELLA DEMCZUK FOR THE NEW YORK TIMES

President Trump entering a rally on Tuesday in Charleston, W.Va., where his promises to support the coal industry have been popular even though his administration predicts its continued decline.

THE BIG PICTURE: COAL IS DYING

The E.P.A. is planning to repeal the Obama administration's Clean Power Plan, which was originally conceived as a sweeping climate change regulation that would push electric utilities to move away from coal and toward cleaner gas and renewables in order to cut carbon dioxide emissions.

In its place, the agency will propose a looser rule that merely encourages coal plants to make modest efficiency upgrades and allows states to regulate carbon dioxide emissions from power plants lightly, if at all.

On paper, that's a drastic revision. But the truth is that utilities had already been shifting away from coal anyway, finding cleaner gas, wind and solar to be more attractive investments. The Clean Power Plan, which was fiercely opposed by industry groups when it was proposed in 2014 and never took effect, was quickly being outpaced by market forces.

The Trump administration's numbers bear this out. In its analysis of the new proposal, the E.P.A. estimated that the total amount of electricity produced by America's coal plants would decline about 23 percent below today's levels by 2030 without any climate regulations at all.

If the Clean Power Plan had taken effect, coal generation would have dropped somewhat more: 29 percent below today's levels.

And if the Trump administration's proposal is finalized? Coal-fired electricity will still decline by roughly 20 percent by 2030, the E.P.A. predicted. The total amount of coal mined for electricity would drop by one-third, compared with levels that are already the lowest in decades.

Consider the case of Ohio-based American Electric Power, one of the nation's largest utilities, which opposed the Clean Power Plan, calling it onerous. The company is nonetheless planning to sharply reduce its reliance on coal, from half its energy mix down to one-third in the next decade, while investing heavily in wind and solar.

"I think this new rule will have a relatively small impact on what we see as our business strategy going forward," said John McManus, senior vice president of environmental services at A.E.P. He noted that the company aimed to cut emissions another 16 percent by 2030 and was planning for the possibility that Congress might eventually enact stronger climate policies, such as a carbon tax.

"We don't expect the climate issue to go away, so we do want to plan for a range of possible futures beyond this particular plan," he added, referring to the E.P.A.'s latest proposal.

A SECOND LIFE FOR SOME PLANTS

The Trump administration's new proposal could, however, offer a reprieve for some individual coal plants around the country.

The majority of the nation's coal-fired power plants are at least 40 years old, and many utilities are currently faced with the choice of paying for upgrades to keep them running or shutting them down.

Under an existing E.P.A. program known as New Source Review, plant owners typically have to install state-of-the-art pollution controls if they significantly upgrade those plants. That acts as a deterrent for keeping those plants open, especially if, say, building a new gas plant might be cheaper.

The Trump administration proposal, for its part, would exempt coal plants from New Source Review if they invest in efficiency improvements under the rule. That could shift the calculus and convince some plant owners to keep their coal plants open longer, especially in states like Kentucky or Wyoming, where there is somewhat less competition from natural gas.

"I wouldn't expect a large number of plants to do this," said Travis Kavulla, the vice chairman of the Montana Public Service Commission. "But you could see this dynamic in regulated electricity markets, where utilities can recover their costs from ratepayers and regulators might be reluctant to close down plants early."

These more efficient coal plants could, in theory, expand their market share. But since coal is the most polluting form of electricity, that would come at a cost: The E.P.A.'s analysis suggests that the resulting increase in particulate pollution, which is linked to heart and lung disease, could cause hundreds of additional premature deaths if the rule keeps more coal plants open.

Still, it is unclear how many plants will pursue this course. Mr. McManus said that A.E.P., which operates in 11 states, may consider upgrading some of its coal plants, but much will depend on whether the rule survives legal review — environmentalists are certain to challenge the revisions to New Source Review in court — and what types of plans states decide to craft.

A BIGGER BAILOUT AHEAD?

Even as coal industry groups cheered the Trump administration's latest move, they also argued that coal plants would likely need further policy support to avert a serious decline.

“These changes to environmental rules are necessary but insufficient,” said Michelle Bloodworth, president of the American Coalition for Clean Coal Electricity, who estimated that roughly 10 percent of the nation’s coal fleet is still on track to retire in the next three years.

One possibility? The Department of Energy is considering a plan that would force grid operators to buy electricity from struggling coal plants (as well as nuclear plants) in order to keep them afloat, using emergency powers normally reserved for exceptional crises like natural disasters.

That rumored move has already drawn criticism from other energy companies, which have called the proposal “legally indefensible” and argue that it would force consumers to pay billions more for electricity. Yet Mr. Trump has urged Energy Secretary Rick Perry to do everything he can to stop plant closings.

CHAPTER 5

Nuclear Energy and Its Risks

Because of its association with nuclear weapons and safety concerns around radiation leakage, public opinion of nuclear power has always wavered. Radiation is invisible and deadly; stories around power plant failures are lurid and scary; nuclear waste byproducts are contaminated. Nuclear power has become much more economical since it was first invented, so cost has tended to override worry. But as these articles express, there is always an ambivalence around nuclear power plants, despite innovative and efficient new power plant design. Even with all the best engineering and science, when nuclear power plants leak, fail or melt down, the effects are catastrophic.

Scientists Warn Atom Power Foes

BY NANCY HICKS | AUG. 16, 1970

UNITED NATIONS, N. Y. — An international gathering of scientists and businessmen concerned with atomic energy in effect told an increasingly hostile public this week that it would have to choose between air-conditioners, dishwashers, television sets and garbage disposals on the one hand and, on the other, greater responsibility for the effects — notably environmental pollution — of increased power demands.

This view emerged from an international symposium, Environmental Aspects of Nuclear Power Stations, at the United Nations.

About 400 representatives of science and industry from 25 countries — all committed to the future of atomic energy as a source of power — attended the meeting, which was sponsored jointly by the International Atomic Energy Agency and the U. S. Atomic Energy Commission.

They met daily, exchanging papers that asserted the relative safety of nuclear energy. They were quick to reply to charges that they excluded any opposing points of view from the meeting.

POWER PLANT DISPUTE

Over the last year and a half, in a time of rising demand for electric power, public opposition to nuclear power plants skyrocketed as the future sanctity of the environment became a national issue. Critics have charged that such plants involve hazards of radiation and thermal pollution of water ways. At the same time, resistance to power plants using conventional fuels has risen because of concern over air pollution.

Many scientists involved in research contend that much of the opposition to nuclear power production is based on "stirrer uppers," as one man called them, who do not have facts. Others concede that the public has genuine concern that should be handled honestly. All agree, however, that the future of nuclear power generation as well as that of fossil fuel (oil or coal) or water will not progress without active public participation in planning.

"I'm personally glad that the public is so interested in the problem of nuclear power generation and the environment," mused Dr. John Dunster of the United Kingdom Atomic Energy Authority. "I hope this means more money and more enthusiasm to be more heavily taxed to pay to protect the environment."

In one paper, Dr. Chauncey Starr, dean of the School of Engineering and Applied Science of the University of California at Los Angeles, developed a philosophical approach to deal with the problem of risk-versus-benefits in future atomic energy production.

'TRADE-OFFS' OF RISKS

He said that in all of American activities there are "trade offs" between risks and acceptability.

"There are contradictory assumptions in the operations of our society," he said. "First, it is commonly accepted that everyone should have the opportunity for a natural death. Second, it is commonly accepted that every individual should have an opportunity to use and enjoy the fruits of our centuries of technological development.

"Third, it is the philosophy of an egalitarian society that where the activities of an individual infringe on others in an undesirable way, the society may intervene to control individual activities in order to achieve a balance between group well-being and the privileges of the individual. It is evident that these inherent assumptions are not compatible."

He added that the risks that the American public was willing to take in sports and transportation was about statistically equal to the death rate caused by disease. He suggested this might be a yardstick to use in determining the probable safety of controversial, risk-benefit questions involved in atomic energy safety, contraceptive pills and the like.

Some scientists, however, have said that these problems of long-range risk are not realistic because nuclear power is just a stopgap measure until some method can be found to harness solar energy, an infinite source, for electric energy production.

Nuclear Power Arrives — Again

BY GENE SMITH | NOV. 29, 1970

"IT'S BEEN A helluva good year for nuclear power," Ellis T. Cox said last week.

Howard M. Winterson agreed. And so did Dr. A. Eugene Shubert and Joseph C. Rengel. The four are the leading competitors in the big business of making nuclear power plants and equipment. Mr. Cox is vice president of the power generation division of the Babcock & Wilcox Company; Mr. Winterson, vice president of the combustion division of Combustion Engineering, Inc.; Dr. Shubert, vice president of the nuclear energy division of the General Electric Company, and Mr. Rengel, executive vice president of the nuclear energy systems division of the Westinghouse Electric Corporation.

To date this year, the domestic electric utilities have placed orders for 16 nuclear power plants with a total capacity of 16,687,000 kilowatts. This is already the third largest year to date and may even move to second best if several pending orders are awarded before Dec. 31.

The best year to date was 1967 when utilities bought 29 nuclear power plants with a total capacity of 25,300,000 kilowatts. A year earlier the totals were 24 plants and 19,500,000 kilowatts of capacity.

But the ordering pace slowed down to a trickle in 1968 as only 10 orders were placed for some 8,845,000 kilowatts. Last year the doldrums continued — eight orders for 8,088,000 kilowatts — as many utilities postponed their purchases because of a combination of disillusionment over delays in building plants laid to labor problems and the opposition of environmentalists and others.

Such obstructions seemed to have little effect on orders this year, due mainly to the problems of dwindling supplies of fossil fuels — coal, oil or gas; the lack of sulphur-free or low pollutant content coal and oil, and rising prices of all but nuclear fuels.

Many in the industry feel that when the Tennessee Valley Authority ordered four giant nuclear plants — two each from Westinghouse and Babcock & Wilcox — because of its inability to secure long-term coal deliveries, other utilities decided it best to consider nuclear power again.

Mr. Rengel pointed out that while capital costs for nuclear plants have soared — about 140 per cent between 1966 and 1970, according to Dr. Glenn Seaborg, chairman of the Atomic Energy Commission — many utilities have found that the reduction of nuclear fuel prices more than compensates for the initial capital charges.

"Let's face it, electric utilities are now faced with gas that will become absolutely unavailable in the long term," Mr. Rengel said. "Oil prices keep rising as air pollution requirements stiffen and no one can even guess where coal prices will top out."

Both he and James Birle, manager of marketing for G. E.'s atomic power equipment department, reported that they had been approached by utilities in Texas and other areas of the Southwest that are now looking into the possibility of building nuclear plants.

"Even in the gas producing regions, they're beginning to worry about fuel supplies," Mr. Birle added.

There are 17 nuclear power plants operating in the United States. Two others, the Monticello plant owned by Northern States Power Company in Minnesota and the Palisades plant of the Consumers Power Company in Michigan, are operable but have been held up pending the outcome of hearings instituted by environmentalists.

Mr. Birle believes that eventually the environmentalists will support nuclear power as the best means of generating electricity with the least possible harm to the environment.

"The general public is very much confused over nuclear power," Mr. Birle said in a telephone interview last week. "With nuclear we have a split in the academic community that is almost unique. This creates confusion in the public mind but we firmly believe that the views of scientists supporting nuclear power will prevail.

"Once the general public analyzes the need for improving living standards and that solutions to urban ills — transportation, sewage, water and air purification — can best be achieved through electricity, nuclear power will win out."

One effect of the potential public opposition to nuclear power plants has been that utilities place their orders some two or three years earlier than load forecasts dictate, thus allowing time for prolonged delays.

Dr. Shubert added that this practice would also develop with conventional fossil-fueled plants as the public demands safeguards before allowing utilities to tamper with land or water in building their plants or rights-of-way.

G. E. leads the atomic sweepstakes both in orders this year and in the cumulative total. To date this year the company has received orders for six plants with a total capacity of some 6 million kilowatts. Combustion Engineering has four with a total capacity of some 4.3 million kilowatts. Westinghouse has received a like number, including one for Puerto Rico, with some 3.7 million kilowatts. Babcock & Wilcox, which has been plagued with a backlog of unfilled orders, received only two plant orders this year with a total capacity of 2.5 million kilowatts.

Mr. Winterson said there is "a reasonably good chance that there will be at least one and possibly two major nuclear plant orders before year-end." The Pacific Gas and Electric Company is expected to decide on a 1.1 million kilowatt plant and the South Carolina Electric and Gas Company is working on an order for a plant of about 800,000 kilowatts.

G. E. recently released a summary of all nuclear power plants ordered through last Oct. 14 by utilities in the United States and abroad. It showed G. E. with a total of 42 domestic and 13 foreign plants for a total of 40,346,000 kilowatts and 40.5 per cent of the market.

Westinghouse was second with 37 domestic and 11 foreign plants totaling 36,165, 000 kilowatts and a 36.2 per cent share.

Babcock & Wilcox with 14 domestic plants rated at 11,751,000 kilowatts was third with an 11.8 per cent slice. Combustion Engineering was a close fourth with 12 plants and 11,023,000 kilowatts for 11 per cent. The Gulf-General Atomics division of the Gulf Oil Corporation has received two domestic orders for a total of 350,000 kilowatts and a 0.5 per cent market share.

"We're basing our planning on an expected total of four plants next year and estimate the industry will order between 16 million and 20 million kilowatts of nuclear plants again in 1971," Mr. Cox said, adding:

"Nineteen seventy-one will be a function of how well we handle our public information for the nuclear industry. We'll have to tell our story on a level of intelligence that will reach the man on the street who is being inflamed by professional intervenors."

Mr. Winterson agrees that 1971 should be about the same level as this year "if the price of fossil fuels keeps escalating."

"Next year should be between 20 million and 25 million kilowatts, or as good or better than this year," Mr. Rengel predicted.

"We started 1970 as the only ones who were really optimistic," Dr. Shubert and Mr. Birle said. "We think 1971 will be substantially better and may even exceed 1967."

Role of Nuclear Power Is Disputed Despite Looming Energy Shortage

SPECIAL TO THE NEW YORK TIMES | JAN. 2, 1990

AS THE 1990'S BEGIN, the nuclear power industry and its most vocal critics agree that the United States faces a new energy shortage, but they remain at odds over the role that nuclear power should play in averting a crisis.

In a report assessing nuclear power in the last decade, environmental groups contend that the industry has not proven it can stand on its own economically or deal with the problems of safety and waste disposal.

The report, "A Decade of Decline: The Degeneration of Nuclear Power in the 1980's and the Emergence of Safer Energy Alternatives," was made public on Thursday. It was prepared by Ralph Nader's Public Citizen organization on behalf of several dozen environmental and anti-nuclear power groups around the country.

NEW FUEL SHORTAGE LOOMS

The makings of an energy shortage in the new decade are not in dispute. Domestic oil production has fallen 13 percent since the Arab oil embargo in 1973, and oil imports have taken up the slack. Moreover, the possibility of global warming, which is caused by the burning of fossil fuels and depletes the ozone layer, poses a potential threat to the environment and could force the nation to restrict the use of oil, coal and natural gas.

"The nuclear industry is now seeking to exploit this situation by portraying itself as the solution to the nation's energy and environmental woes," the report said. Despite the promises of nuclear power, critics contend, the industry has grown more costly, safety has not improved and the problem of radioactive waste has not been solved.

Responding to the report, proponents of nuclear plants said in interviews that as the cost of imported oil rises and domestic production shrinks, the industry will become more competitive and part of the solution to the energy crisis.

But serious obstacles remain. In the last decade there were no orders for new nuclear reactors. Documents obtained from the Nuclear Regulatory Commission and the Department of Energy show that eight licensed reactors were closed and 60 that had been ordered or were under construction were cancelled.

At the same time the cost of construction for new plants, not accounting for inflation, rose from $1,135 per kilowatt in 1980 to $4,590 in 1989, the report said. The cost of most "renewable" sources of energy, like hydroelectric, solar and wind power, declined, and their electric generating capacity grew by 27 percent, producing more power than nuclear plants.

NEW PLANTS SAID TO BE CHEAPER

But industry officials say that the financial picture is improving and that in some cases nuclear power is cheaper than other sources.

"Of course, the viable option is going to depend upon economics," said Richard Slember, vice president of Energy Systems at the Westinghouse Corporation, one of the nation's largest manufacturers of commercial nuclear reactors. The current generation of plants is cheaper, more efficient and much safer than previous designs, Mr. Slember said.

Plants that began operating in the 1980's were expensive because of high interest rates, exorbitant construction costs and new safety requirements after the accident at Three Mile Island plant in Pennsylvania, said Cathy Steel Roche, media director at the United States Council for Energy Awareness, the industry's main trade organization. "With those costs now under control, our belief is that nuclear power will be economically competitive."

The major stumbling block to the wider use of nuclear power, the

BETTMANN/GETTY IMAGES

Three Mile Island Nuclear Power Plant on March 30, 1979, two days after a meltdown that forced the closure of the plant.

industry contends, is not the plants but the regulatory process that has forced them to sit idle.

"It's going to take some sort of crisis," said John Sillin of the Management Analysis Company in Washington, a consulting firm to the nuclear industry. "The state licensing commissions will only come around when the brownouts continue and get worse."

But the report said the public is most concerned because it thinks the plants are neither safe nor reliable. Indeed, public support for nuclear power withered after the incidents at Three Mile Island and Chernobyl in the Soviet Union.

Nuclear Fallout

OPINION | BY KRISTEN IVERSEN | MARCH 10, 2012

I GREW UP IN Arvada, Colo., in the shadow of a nuclear bomb factory, so I read the just-released report on the Fukushima meltdown in Japan with special interest. Coinciding with the first anniversary of the Fukushima Daiichi disaster, the 400-page report details the extensive misinformation supplied to the public by the Tokyo Electric Power Company (Tepco) in collusion with Japanese officials.

The Japanese government's failure to warn citizens about radioactive danger put the entire city of Tokyo at health risk — and the rest of us as well. The report, which was written by an independent investigative panel established by the Rebuild Japan Initiative Foundation (published March 1 in the Bulletin of the Atomic Scientists), bluntly states that the much vaunted "absolute safety" of nuclear power is no more than a "twisted myth."

The threat from nuclear power plants is twofold: grand scale catastrophe and continuing health problems connected with radioactive contamination in our air, water, soil and food supply — both short-term, high-level contamination and the long-term, low-level kind.

In Japan, radiation was detected in beef, milk, spinach, tea leaves and rice. And more than a dozen cities in the United States tested positive for fallout from Fukushima in their water supplies. Scientists found radiation from Japan in milk from Phoenix to Little Rock, Ark., to Montpelier, Vt. A year later, many questions about Fukushima's operations remain unanswered.

Tepco may be the latest in a line of the nuclear businesses with a self-imposed mandate to suppress truth. Here in the United States, we have our own tightly held radioactive secrets.

Rocky Flats, the now notorious Colorado bomb factory, produced plutonium "triggers" for nuclear weapons in the United States from 1952 to 1989. There were countless fires, leaks and accidents at Rocky

Flats; after decades of weapons production, and little environmental oversight, the area was profoundly contaminated.

During my childhood, none of us knew exactly what the plant actually did; the rumor in the neighborhood was that it made household cleaning products. We knew nothing about the 5,000 tainted barrels that leaked plutonium into the soil. Nor did we know about the two large fires, in 1957 and 1969, that sent radioactive plumes over the Denver metro area. Wind and water carried toxic elements into surrounding neighborhoods, including mine. The public was never warned. Energy Department studies confirm that plutonium, carbon tetrachloride and other radioactive and toxic contaminants routinely escaped from the plant. Although the plant closed more than 20 years ago, a recent study suggests that plutonium may still be migrating into neighboring areas. The connection between Fukushima and Rocky Flats was made explicit when recent soil tests for offsite plutonium at Rocky Flats found cesium — from Fukushima.

I worked at Rocky Flats but didn't realize what kind of risks the plant posed until a 1994 "Nightline" special informed me I was working next to 14 tons of plutonium, most of it unsafely stored.

One man tried to sound an alarm. Dr. Carl Johnson, Jefferson County health director from 1973 to 1981, directed numerous studies on contamination levels and health risks the plant posed to public health. Based on his conclusions, Dr. Johnson opposed housing development near Rocky Flats. He was fired. Later studies confirmed many of his findings.

The government and private operators of Rocky Flats say that there's been no harm to local residents and that the plutonium that has escaped from the plant — potentially as much as three tons over nearly four decades — is harmless. It's no greater than "a pinch of salt and pepper," Edward Putzier, the health physics manager for Dow Chemical, which used to operate Rocky Flats, told a civic group in 1971 . One difference between salt and pepper and plutonium is that one-millionth of a gram of plutonium, if inhaled or ingested, can cause cancer. Also plutonium, unlike salt or pepper, is invisible.

Rocky Flats was in my backyard, but our collective backyard — from Tokyo to Cincinnati to Denver to Benton County, Wash., home of Hanford, which housed nine nuclear reactors and is now one of the most heavily contaminated places on earth — is under similar threat. Interestingly, in 1991 when Congress approved closure of Fernald, an Ohio uranium processing facility, federal scientists conceded that no one could ever safely live there, and that the site would have to be closely monitored forever. The only absolute is the potential for tragedy.

Yet President Obama supports investment in nuclear energy, including two new nuclear power plants in Georgia. The National Nuclear Security Administration wants to build a new facility to increase trigger production at Los Alamos National Laboratory, in New Mexico. And in Colorado there's a big push to build a highway and expand business and residential development on contaminated land. In spite of everything we've learned, profit continues to trump safety.

In 1995, the Department of Energy said it would take 50 years and $37 billion to clean up Rocky Flats, and it wasn't sure the technology existed to do the job. The D.O.E. later awarded a $3.5 billion contract to Kaiser-Hill to clean up the site.

The Energy Department based the standards for the cleanup project on the exposure level of a wildlife refuge worker rather than families and children. Now, despite public opposition, the Rocky Flats nuclear weapons facility is the Rocky Flats National Wildlife Refuge. Except for the 1,300-acre portion of the site so drenched in plutonium that federal and state officials say it is not safe for human activity.

Rocky Flats is a beautiful area, with great mountain views, and supplies a perfect setting in which to reflect on nuclear safety and other twisted mythologies.

KRISTEN IVERSEN is the director of the M.F.A. program at the University of Memphis, and author of the forthcoming "Full Body Burden: Growing Up in the Nuclear Shadow of Rocky Flats."

Nuclear Power's Death Somewhat Exaggerated

BY MATTHEW L. WALD | APRIL 10, 2012

NUCLEAR ENERGY IS going through an odd patch. It refuses to die, but it does not prosper.

This is how modest the nuclear industry's prospects now look: Senator Lamar Alexander, a Tennessee Republican who has called for building 100 reactors in the next few years, told a conference of industry specialists in late March that the long-ballyhooed "nuclear renaissance" did not really exist anymore. Now, he said, it is an "awakening to the awareness of nuclear."

But it is an awakening with a price of $30 billion or more. Mr. Alexander was speaking to a conference convened on the 33rd anniversary of the Three Mile Island accident, a few weeks after the Nuclear Regulatory Commission gave permission to build a power reactor for the first time in more than 30 years, for the twin Vogtle reactors near Augusta, Ga.

Those will cost $14 billion, if all goes well, and more if it does not. A few days after he spoke, the commission approved a license for another pair of reactors in South Carolina, which will cost about the same. Several other companies are laying out hundreds of millions of dollars in planning for reactors that may or may not get to the groundbreaking stage.

The industry's three great recent stumbling blocks, the Fukushima accident of March 2011, the exceptionally low price of natural gas and a recession that has stunted demand for power, mock the idea that dozens of new reactors are waiting in the wings. But in an era of worry over global warming, support is plentiful for at least keeping a toe in the water.

"Even if global warming science was not explicitly invented by the nuclear lobby, the science could hardly suit the lobby better," complained a book published last month, "The Doomsday Machine," a polemic on the evils of splitting the atom. In fact, the industry continues to argue that in the United States it is by far the largest source of zero-carbon energy, and recently began a campaign of upbeat ads to improve its image.

According to the authors of "The Doomsday Machine," Martin Cohen and Andrew McKillop, "In almost every country — usually for reasons completely unrelated to its ability to deliver electricity — there is almost universal political support for nuclear power."

That is probably an exaggeration, with Japan leaving almost all of its 54 reactors idle at the moment because of the Fukushima Daiichi triple meltdown, and Germany promising to close its fleet. But China and India, two countries with enormous demand for electricity and not much hand-wringing over global warming, are planning huge reactor construction projects.

And even the Japanese catastrophe plays in some quarters as a reason to build new reactors. For example, the reactors being built in Georgia and South Carolina are the AP1000 model, with the letters standing for "advanced passive," because emergency cooling relies on natural forces like gravity, evaporation and convection, not power-operated pumps and valves that require a supply of electricity, the force that Fukushima simply did not have.

At the same conference that Senator Alexander addressed, Jim Ferland, then the president and chief executive of Westinghouse Electric, insisted, "If an AP1000 had been there, we wouldn't be having this discussion today; that plant would be back on line." General Electric, which designed the reactors used by Tokyo Electric Power at Fukushima, has made similar claims for its new "passively safe" design.

If the nation's 104 reactors, all but one finished by the 1980s, were eventually replaced, it would be with equipment that has fewer moving parts and fewer ways to get into accidents. But they may not be replaced because the competition from other sources of electricity is strong.

In the United States, nuclear power is stumbling forward because of an energy policy of limited diversity — what President Obama refers to as his “all of the above” strategy. That means loan guarantees and production tax credits for new reactors, created in the George W. Bush administration, are viewed favorably in the Obama White House. But “all of the above” also means support for solar and wind, as well as support for oil and natural gas production, especially hydraulic fracturing for gas in shale rock.

Fracking, as it is known, has turned gas into a formidable competitor. Gas is priced in a unit called a million B.T.U.’s, a quantity that will produce about 150 kilowatt-hours, about as much as a small house uses in a week.

When gas was $14 per million B.T.U.’s, it cost 9 cents per kilowatt-hour just for the fuel. Today, with natural gas priced at about $3 per million B.T.U.’s, the fuel cost to make a kilowatt-hour is about 2 cents. That does not count the cost of building the plant to burn the gas, but it does make almost anything else, including zero-carbon sources like solar, wind and nuclear, much less attractive.

In the wings are other competitors, including the possibility of a better reactor. The Energy Department recently said it might spend $450 million on “small modular reactors” that could be built in a factory and trucked to sites to replace old coal plants or power small communities. The government, though, researches far more types of reactors than ever achieve commercial life.

And the Fukushima meltdowns did not help. “It seems like every time something happens, you always get these prognostications this is the end, the nuclear industry has come to a halt,” said William D. Magwood IV, one of the five members of the Nuclear Regulatory Commission and a former assistant secretary of energy in charge of promoting nuclear power.

Fukushima, said Bart Gordon, a former Democratic representative from Tennessee and former chairman of the House Committee on Science, Space and Technology, was “undermining some of the environmental converts, so the political issue is more difficult.”

Fukushima certainly did not help the South Texas Project expansion, one of the four selected by the Energy Department as prime candidates for loan guarantees. That project was in trouble before March 2011, because an important municipal partner had dropped out.

One of the replacement partners was the Tokyo Electric Power Company, which is now hardly in a position to invest in new reactors abroad. Another candidate for a loan guarantee, now probably dead, was the Calvert Cliffs 3 project, about 40 miles south of Washington, which was supposed to be built in a competitive marketplace, where the price of power was set by natural gas. That made even the Energy Department rather skeptical about its prospects.

Mr. Magwood argues that the situation is not so dire, though, because the "renaissance" was never as big as some people assumed. He said he calculated in 2008 that of the 23 or so projects that were under discussion, only 12 were actually under development, and of those, only 10 faced no real licensing or technical hurdles. But only five of those had clear sources of financing. He assumed three would be in the first wave; now it is two. The industry insists that even its small-scale rebirth is a step forward. Those two pairs of reactors could lay the groundwork for more.

Mr. Ferland said that AP1000s in this country would be easier to build because of the experience of construction in China. For example, he said, technicians there had misrigged one heavy component at a plant, bending it slightly and causing a two-week delay. That will not happen in Georgia or South Carolina, he said. Smaller lessons, like how to lay out cable trays so they do not occupy space later needed for other components, were accumulating rapidly, he said.

Simply breaking ground on a reactor and finishing it, something this country has not done for 30 years, would be a step forward.

U.S. Acts to Spur Development of High-Tech Reactors

BY HENRY FOUNTAIN | JAN. 19, 2016

THE OBAMA ADMINISTRATION is providing seed money for two advanced nuclear reactor designs, part of its effort to keep nuclear power in the nation's energy mix over the next several decades.

The Energy Department said it would provide up to $40 million each to two companies, X-energy and Southern Company, over about five years to help develop the alternative reactor designs. As a start, the department, which announced the investments last Friday, is giving each company $6 million this year.

Nuclear energy, which produces practically no greenhouse gas emissions, accounts for 19 percent of the electricity produced in the United States. But safety and radioactive waste handling have long been issues, and in recent years abundant, inexpensive natural gas has disrupted the economics of energy production, making some nuclear plants unprofitable. A few plants have been closed and only five new plants are under construction.

The Energy Department has worked to extend the operating lifetime of existing plants for 20 years beyond their original 40-year licenses. Even so, without further licensing extensions, many of the nation's 99 operating plants will have to shut down by 2030.

The government has been helping to finance research on new reactor designs for years, but as yet no designs have reached the market. The department expects that a type called small modular reactors will be the first new designs to begin operating, in the mid-2020s.

These reactors are smaller but use the same basic technologies as current plants. They can be built in factories, reducing costs, and although they produce far less power than large plants, units can be added as needed.

The financing announced last week by the energy secretary, Ernest Moniz, is for even more advanced technologies that may not be deployed until the mid-2030s at the earliest. In addition to electricity production, some of these advanced reactors could be used for other industrial processes, including desalination.

X-energy is working on a so-called pebble bed reactor, in which the uranium fuel is contained in ceramic- and graphite-covered balls rather than long, thin rods, and is cooled by gas rather than water. In such a design, the fuel cannot melt down in an accident, so a reactor should be able to be safely located close to population centers.

Southern is working with TerraPower and research groups on a design that uses molten chloride, which acts as both coolant and as the medium for the fuel. The material is designed to be self-cooling in an accident, without the need for emergency water cooling systems.

The Obama administration has made preserving and expanding nuclear power a major component of its plan to reduce energy emissions to fight climate change. But on nuclear power the United States is in some ways behind China, which is aggressively building new large plants and has also begun building a small modular reactor in Shandong Province, between Beijing and Shanghai.

Last week the state-owned China General Nuclear Power Corporation announced that it had received approval to build a small floating nuclear reactor as a demonstration project. A floating reactor has some advantages over land-based units, including ready access to cooling water. Such a reactor could also be dismantled more easily, by being transported to a special decommissioning facility.

CHAPTER 6

The Future: Energy and Policy Innovations

Energy production and consumption continues to see radical innovations, from ever-deeper deepwater drilling for oil, to more efficient solar and wind farms, to electric cars that one day will be ubiquitous. These innovations will have material effects on geopolitical power dynamics as well as how we live our daily lives.

New Technologies Redraw the World's Energy Picture

BY CLIFFORD KRAUSS | OCT. 25, 2011

GOLDA MEIR, THE former prime minister of Israel, used to tell a joke about how Moses must have made a wrong turn in the desert: "He dragged us 40 years through the desert to bring us to the one place in the Middle East where there was no oil."

As it turns out, Moses may have had it right all along. In the last couple of years, vast amounts of natural gas have been found deep under Israel's Mediterranean waters, and studies have begun to test the feasibility of extracting synthetic oil from a large kerogen-rich rock field southwest of Jerusalem.

Israel's swing of fate is just one of many big energy surprises developing as a new generation of unconventional fossil fuels take hold.

From the high Arctic waters north of Norway to a shale field in Argentine Patagonia, from the oil sands of western Canada to deepwater oil prospects off the shores of Angola, giant new oil and gas fields are being mined, steamed and drilled with new technologies. Some of the reserves have been known to exist for decades but were inaccessible either economically or technologically.

Put together, these fuels should bring hundreds of billions of barrels of recoverable reserves to market in coming decades and shift geopolitical and economic calculations around the world. The new drilling boom is expected to diversify global sources away from the Middle East, just as the growth in consumption of fuels shifts from the United States and Europe to China, India and the rest of the developing world.

"Use whatever hackneyed phrase you want, like tectonic shift or game-changer," said Edward L. Morse, global head of commodity research at Citigroup. "These sources will dramatically change the energy supply outlook, and there is little debate about that."

This striking shift in energy started in the 1990s with the first deepwater wells in the Gulf of Mexico and Brazil, but it has taken off in the last decade as a result of declining conventional fields, climbing energy prices and swift technological change.

The United States may now have the means to reduce its half century of dependence on the Middle East. China and India may have the means to fuel the development of their growing middle classes. Japan and much of Europe may have the chance to reduce dependence on nuclear power. And, at least theoretically, poor African countries might be able to lift themselves out of poverty.

For consumers around the world, the new fuels should moderate future price increases.

But giving new life to fossil fuels is a devil's bargain, probably making solutions to climate change, and the development of renewable energy, even more difficult. "Not only are you extending the fossil fuels era," said Daniel Lashof, director of the climate program at the Natural Resources Defense Council, "but you are moving into fossil fuels that are dirtier and release more carbon pollution in the process of extracting and using them."

James Burkhard, a managing director of the energy consulting firm IHS Cera, said that competition between fossil fuels and renewable energy development was driven by the price of oil and gas as well as by government policy.

"The unconventional boom will guarantee that the competition is strong for years to come," Mr. Burkhard said. "If oil costs $200 a barrel, that would provide more headroom for electric vehicles. But if oil is at $90, alternative, renewable energy will need to compete better on an economic basis."

THE DEEPWATER RESERVES

The future is now when it comes to deepwater offshore drilling, which has already measurably increased oil and gas supplies around the world.

In 2000, fewer than 20 vessels in the world could drill deepwater wells. Now there are nearly 200, and more almost every month. Global deepwater oil production leapt to roughly seven million barrels a day in the last 11 years, up from 1.5 million barrels, and now provides about 8 percent of the world's oil supply. That production could double by 2020, according to experts.

Most of the drilling is in the Gulf of Mexico, off Brazil, Australia and India, and along the west coast of Africa. But only about 10 percent of the world's deepwater oil and gas fields have been extensively explored and drilled.

In recent years, advances in computer processing power have allowed geologists to make sense of seismic data 15,000 feet or more below the ocean floor. Three-dimensional imaging and seismic mapping are now possible even below thick layers of salt, which used to blur views of untapped reservoirs. Superstrong alloys allow drill bits to go into hot, high-pressure fields.

Even with the advances, risks remain, as the BP Deepwater Horizon disaster last year demonstrated. Regulations became somewhat tougher worldwide, yet they caused little more than a pause in drilling. Even in the United States, drilling was almost back to pre-Horizon levels a year after the accident.

Cuba is planning to start drilling exploratory wells offshore at the end of the year, and Mexico is slowly moving toward deepwater drilling to revive its flagging oil industry. Drilling has begun in the deep waters off Ghana, and experts say they believe fertile fields exist all the way down the west coast of Africa to Namibia. The potential for new wealth could give Africa a better chance for development, although the history of Nigerian oil development is a cautionary tale of corruption, environmental degradation and strife.

Geologists say they believe the fields of West Africa fit like jigsaw puzzle pieces with prospective fields in South America, because the two continents were connected hundreds of millions of years ago. Total and Royal Dutch Shell recently made a major discovery along the coast of French Guiana, and neighboring Suriname is likely to become an important producer, too. Some analysts say they think more offshore fields may be discovered along the Brazilian coast and south to Argentina.

The coasts of East Africa are rich in gas, and China, Indonesia, Malaysia, Australia and the Philippines also have significant deepwater potential. And India's deepwater prospects could provide much of its gas needs as its economy grows.

"We are just at the beginning of this story," said William Colton, Exxon Mobil's vice president for strategic planning. "It's only likely we will find more deepwater resources."

OIL SANDS

Oil sands have already transformed Canada into an energy superpower, and they have shifted American dependency from the nations of the Organization of the Petroleum Exporting Countries to a friendlier and more stable source. Oil sands have been around for decades, but they were too expensive to produce at large scale. Then rising oil prices altered the economics in their favor — attracting multibillion-dollar investments from international oil companies, including those in China.

Since 2000, production has expanded to more than 1.5 million barrels a day of synthetic oil from 600,000, making Canada's oil sands the most important source of oil imported to the United States. (Canada also exports considerable conventional oil to the United States.)

"It's one thing to find oil, and another thing to find oil in a very safe, secure place like Canada," said Mr. Colton of Exxon Mobil. "From a U.S. energy security standpoint, it's a very attractive proposition to U.S. consumers that we have this friend next door who has all these oil resources."

Canadian oil sands production is expected to increase by as much as 200,000 barrels a day every year for the next two decades. Current estimates of how much is there already top Iraq's total reserves, guaranteeing Canada's place as a premier oil producer for many decades. IHS Cera projects $100 billion in investments in the oil sands over the next decade.

The only thing holding back production of Canada's oil sands are environmental concerns. Much of the oil sands come from carving mining sites out of large sections of the boreal forest, an important depository for containing carbon and a breeding ground for many bird species. Refining of the oil sands, which requires the burning of natural gas, is more carbon-intensive than refining of most other crude oils, despite a 40 percent reduction since 1990 in carbon emissions for each barrel produced.

Technological improvements in recent years have streamlined the burdensome refining process for bitumen, the feedstock in synthetic oil production. Recovering reserves from deeper underground using steam injection, rather than mining, has reduced the footprint of operations and some environmental damage to the forests.

But opposition remains strong among American and Canadian environmentalists, who are fighting to stop pipelines to the United

States and western Canadian ports. Without those pipelines, oil sands production capacity would most likely struggle to grow. That resistance has forced the oil companies to invest heavily in research to reduce the footprint of extraction and carbon emissions.

The Obama administration has been considering a proposed 1,711-mile, $7 billion pipeline to connect Canada's oil sands production to terminals in Oklahoma and refineries on the Gulf Coast. The State Department recently gave the project a passing grade in an environmental impact statement, increasing the likelihood of approval. With the pipeline, Canada would move an additional 700,000 barrels a day.

The synthetic fuels now go almost entirely to the American and Canadian markets, but China and other Asian countries are increasingly interested in the oil sands. Chinese companies have invested more than $15 billion in Canadian oil sands projects over the last two years, even though there is not yet a way to get the fuel to China.

The Canadian company Enbridge is proposing a pipeline from Alberta to Kitimat, British Columbia, near the coast, where tankers could load for trips to Asia. Sinopec of China is helping to finance the $5.5 billion project. The pipeline could be completed by 2017 but faces various regulatory hurdles and opposition from Native Canadian groups.

China wants to obtain 15 billion to 20 billion additional barrels of foreign oil reserves over the next few years, so it also has its eyes on an enormous heavy oil field in the Orinoco Belt, in the northeast part of Venezuela. Production started in recent years, and several projects that have been announced could produce up to two million barrels a day by 2020.

SHALE

The biggest wild card for the future of oil and gas may be shale and other tight rocks. Finding and producing hydrocarbons from these rocks has taken off in the United States with such velocity that it has already significantly altered government and corporate energy expectations. At the beginning of the last decade, the United States was believed to be burning quickly through its gas resources, and a flurry of construction began to build liquefied natural gas import terminals.

But a surge in production in shale fields across Pennsylvania, Texas, Louisiana and several other states over the last five years has produced such a glut that the price of natural gas has plummeted, and energy companies are proposing to convert their empty import terminals into export facilities.

The new drilling was made possible by a mixture of new and old technologies. Hydraulic fracturing, or fracking — the shooting of water, sand and chemicals at high pressures to fracture hard rock — has been done for decades. Now, combining that practice with horizontal drilling — directionally guiding a drill bit through a shale reservoir, as opposed to conventional vertical drilling — has taken advantage of fields that were practically useless in the past.

Shale gas production in the United States is more than five times as great now as in 2006, and the country surpassed Russia as the world's leading gas producer in 2009.

A variety of environmental groups oppose the surge, saying the chemicals in fracking fluids can pollute water supplies. Temporary or permanent fracking bans have been put in place in New York, New Jersey and Maryland. Other states are toughening drilling regulations, and the industry is responding with tighter wastewater management, while the Environmental Protection Agency is expected to complete a study on fracking next year. Nevertheless, gas shale drilling appears likely to continue at a fast pace in the most important gas-producing states.

The rest of the world is watching. Moratoriums have been put in place in parts of France, Germany, South Africa and the Canadian province of Quebec; Britain, Ukraine and other countries are moving cautiously forward. Still, the Energy Department projects that gas from shale could account for 14 percent of global supplies by 2030, with as many as 32 countries having production potential.

Poland is likely to be the next big shale player, with the government eager to lessen its gas dependence on Russia, which provides half of Poland's energy. Already more than eight million acres have been leased by Chevron, Exxon Mobil, ConocoPhillips and other large international companies. Drilling success in Poland could lead to more drilling in shale fields in Germany, Norway, Sweden, France and Ukraine.

Europe imports about 60 percent of its gas, roughly half of that from Russia. With many Europeans wanting to reduce their energy dependence on coal-fired generation and nuclear power, there should be a strong impetus to increase domestic production, at least in some countries.

China is also moving fast. With a goal of satisfying 10 percent of its gas demand from shale by 2020, it held its first shale gas auction in June. China has a big incentive to develop shale gas, because it is poised to become the world's largest importer of natural gas and it wants to reduce its dependence on coal to clean up the air of its cities.

In the last five years, as engineers advanced their techniques, shales have begun to produce oil as well. The Bakken field in North Dakota and Montana now produces 400,000 barrels a day, up from a trickle in 2007, and oil executives predict production could soar to a million barrels a day by 2015. The first well was drilled in the Eagle Ford shale field in south Texas three years ago; the field now produces more than 100,000 barrels a day, with 420,000 expected by 2015.

There are 20 other shale and similar tight rock fields across the United States that could make states like Ohio and Michigan major producers.

Exploration of such fields outside the United States and Canada is barely in its infancy, although there are major shale fields across Europe, China, Australia, Africa and South America. "It could change production forecasts around the world," said Bobby Ryan, Chevron's vice president for global exploration. "But we are still at the point of the spear. We have to shoot the seismic first to find out."

Chinese, Norwegian and other foreign companies have already entered into joint ventures in shale oil and gas exploration in the United States to learn fracking techniques. China is moving fast to study its shales, although so far there seems to be more gas than oil. Argentina also looks promising for oil and gas, with American companies including Apache, Exxon Mobil and EOG Resources making large investments in shale in the Argentine province of Neuquen.

But there are constraints, including political opposition. Geological analysis of shales globally has barely started, and there are limits to the equipment and skilled manpower available for drilling. This has delayed fracturing jobs and raised costs in developed fields. Africa and the Middle East appear to have promising reserves, and Saudi Arabia has begun studying its shale fields, but the water requirements for fracking will be a high hurdle absent a technological breakthrough.

HIGH ARCTIC

The last frontier, at least for the foreseeable future, is the high Arctic, most of which is still unexplored by oil companies. High winds, months of darkness and icebergs have long stymied dreams of finding vast quantities of oil and gas in the northern reaches of the globe.

A 2008 assessment by the United States Geological Survey estimated that a quarter of the world's remaining undiscovered conventional oil and gas is in the Arctic, more than 80 percent of it in forbidding offshore areas. Again the United States is the big potential winner, with an estimated one-third of the total undiscovered oil, according to the survey.

Large oil and gas discoveries began in Russia and Alaska in the 1960s, and more than 40 fields are now in production across Alaska, Russia, Norway and Canada. Shell has been trying for five years to drill in Alaska's Chukchi and Beaufort Seas and has invested about $4 billion on 10-year leases. But regulatory agencies or courts have delayed its efforts, because of concerns that Arctic waters are vital breeding grounds for many aquatic species that are endangered or at risk and that a well blowout could cause a huge leak that would be difficult or impossible to fix.

A paper released by the national commission on the BP Deepwater Horizon spill warned that a serious leak in the high Arctic would be extremely difficult to clean up. That is partly because skimmers can become clogged in ice and spilled oil is unlikely to degrade in frigid temperatures.

But in August, Shell received conditional approval from the Interior Department to begin drilling exploratory wells next summer. The company estimates that 25 billion barrels of oil are in the Alaskan Arctic, mostly in the Chukchi Sea.

"We're hopeful," said Pete Slaiby, Shell's vice president for Alaska, although the company still faces several regulatory hurdles and perhaps some legal ones, too. As for the rest of the Arctic, Mr. Slaiby acknowledged that drilling would require strong regulatory regimes and large companies with the experience and resources to drill in the most challenging environments.

"I'm confident, but it will require high bars, financial acumen and operational acumen," he said. "You want companies that have financial resources and operational skills to develop the Arctic responsibly. It will be expensive."

Other companies are moving forward in other Arctic countries.

Chevron is doing seismic work in Canada's Arctic waters. Cairn Energy, a British company, has drilled several exploratory wells off Greenland in recent months, so far with little success. Exxon Mobil and Rosneft, a company controlled by the Russian government, have agreed to invest $3.2 billion in exploration in the ice-clogged Kara Sea.

Statoil of Norway and ENI of Italy are furthest along in the far northern waters of Norway, which has the advantage of being ice-free because of warm Gulf Stream waters. Statoil already operates a gas field, called Snow White, 340 miles north of the Arctic Circle in the Barents Sea, and several companies are drilling oil wells in the sea now. The operations accelerated after the discovery of an estimated

250 million barrels of retrievable reserves of high-quality sweet crude oil in the Skrugard field in April, the seventh-largest oil or gas find in the world this year.

"This is the premier next frontier," said Tim Dodson, Statoil's executive vice president for exploration.

POWER BALANCES

While many countries stand to benefit from the new energy resources, the United States may have the most to gain.

Before the 1960s, American companies dominated Persian Gulf and North Africa oil resources and made lasting alliances with autocratic governments. By the 1970s, as the United States' oil production peaked and OPEC and national oil companies took command of the world's oil, the United States had to accept almost hostage status. Now the tables are turning.

"There is the potential to really rebalance strategic power in the world," said David L. Goldwyn, former State Department coordinator for international energy affairs. "If we are able to manage significant incremental supply from Canada, from onshore U.S., from Brazil and friendly countries in West Africa, then we can significantly ameliorate the risk of a supply disruption in the Middle East or from other countries that might use oil as a weapon."

While more energy sources could be a stabilizing factor, competition over the new fields could produce tensions. Already, in the South China Sea, China has warned India's state oil company not to drill in waters it claims. Turkey recently warned Cyprus against drilling for natural gas without reaching an agreement with Turkish Cypriots over royalties. The political twists and turns are bound to be many. The devil's bargain looks like a necessity for the United States, China and many other countries, as the continued extraction and use of fossil fuels will come with some environmental degradation. According to the most recent estimates of the Energy Department, world energy demand is going to increase by 50 percent by 2035, largely because of increased consumption in China, India and the rest of the developing world.

Renewable energy will rise as a percentage of energy used, to 15 percent from 10 percent, but that will not provide for the growing demand.

"The fossil fuel age will be extended for decades," said Ivan Sandrea, president of the Energy Intelligence Group, a research publisher. "Unconventional oil and gas are at the beginning of a technological cycle that can last 60 years. They are really in their infancy."

U.S. Inches Toward Goal of Energy Independence

BY CLIFFORD KRAUSS AND ERIC LIPTON | MARCH 22, 2012

MIDLAND, TEX. — The desolate stretch of West Texas desert known as the Permian Basin is still the lonely domain of scurrying roadrunners by day and howling coyotes by night. But the roar of scores of new oil rigs and the distinctive acrid fumes of drilling equipment are unmistakable signs that crude is gushing again.

And not just here. Across the country, the oil and gas industry is vastly increasing production, reversing two decades of decline. Using new technology and spurred by rising oil prices since the mid-2000s, the industry is extracting millions of barrels more a week, from the deepest waters of the Gulf of Mexico to the prairies of North Dakota.

At the same time, Americans are pumping significantly less gasoline. While that is partly a result of the recession and higher gasoline prices, people are also driving fewer miles and replacing older cars with more fuel-efficient vehicles at a greater clip, federal data show.

Taken together, the increasing production and declining consumption have unexpectedly brought the United States markedly closer to a goal that has tantalized presidents since Richard Nixon: independence from foreign energy sources, a milestone that could reconfigure American foreign policy, the economy and more. In 2011, the country imported just 45 percent of the liquid fuels it used, down from a record high of 60 percent in 2005.

"There is no question that many national security policy makers will believe they have much more flexibility and will think about the world differently if the United States is importing a lot less oil," said Michael A. Levi, an energy and environmental senior fellow at the Council on Foreign Relations. "For decades, consumption rose, production fell and imports increased, and now every one of those trends is going the other way."

JIM WILSON/THE NEW YORK TIMES

An Apache Corporation well near Hobbs, N.M. Apache is drilling in the Permian Basin, an oil field once thought played out.

How the country made this turnabout is a story of industry-friendly policies started by President Bush and largely continued by President Obama — many over the objections of environmental advocates — as well as technological advances that have allowed the extraction of oil and gas once considered too difficult and too expensive to reach. But mainly it is a story of the complex economics of energy, which sometimes seems to operate by its own rules of supply and demand.

With gasoline prices now approaching record highs and politicians mud-wrestling about the causes and solutions, the effects of the longer-term rise in production can be difficult to see.

Simple economics suggests that if the nation is producing more energy, prices should be falling. But crude oil — and gasoline and diesel made from it — are global commodities whose prices are affected by factors around the world. Supply disruptions in Africa, the political standoff with Iran and rising demand from a recovering world economy all are contributing to the current spike in global oil prices, offsetting the impact of the increased domestic supply.

But the domestic trends are unmistakable. Not only has the United States reduced oil imports from members of the Organization of the Petroleum Exporting Countries by more than 20 percent in the last three years, it has become a net exporter of refined petroleum products like gasoline for the first time since the Truman presidency. The natural gas industry, which less than a decade ago feared running out of domestic gas, is suddenly dealing with a glut so vast that import facilities are applying for licenses to export gas to Europe and Asia.

National oil production, which declined steadily to 4.95 million barrels a day in 2008 from 9.6 million in 1970, has risen over the last four years to nearly 5.7 million barrels a day. The Energy Department projects that daily output could reach nearly seven million barrels by 2020. Some experts think it could eventually hit 10 million barrels — which would put the United States in the same league as Saudi Arabia.

This surge is hardly without consequences. Some areas of intense drilling activity, including northeastern Utah and central Wyoming, have experienced air quality problems. The drilling technique called hydraulic fracturing, or fracking, which uses highly pressurized water, sand and chemical lubricants that help force more oil and gas from rock formations, has also been blamed for wastewater problems. Wildlife experts also warn that expanded drilling is threatening habitats of rare or endangered species.

Greater energy independence is "a prize that has long been eyed by oil insiders and policy strategists that can bring many economic and national security benefits," said Jay Hakes, a senior official at the Energy Department during the Clinton administration. "But we will have to work through the environmental issues, which are a definite challenge."

The increased production of fossil fuels is a far cry from the energy plans President Obama articulated as a candidate in 2008. Then, he promoted policies to help combat global warming, including vast investments in renewable energy and a cap-and-trade system for carbon emissions that would have discouraged the use of fossil fuels.

More recently, with gasoline prices rising and another election looming, Mr. Obama has struck a different chord. He has opened new federal lands and waters to drilling, trumpeted increases in oil and gas production and de-emphasized the challenges of climate change. On Thursday, he said he supported expedited construction of the southern portion of the proposed Keystone XL oil pipeline from Canada.

Mr. Obama's current policy has alarmed many environmental advocates who say he has failed to adequately address the environmental threats of expanded drilling and the use of fossil fuels. He also has not silenced critics, including Republicans and oil executives, who accuse him of preventing drilling on millions of acres off the Atlantic and Pacific Coasts and on federal land, unduly delaying the decision on the full Keystone project and diverting scarce federal resources to pie-in-the-sky alternative energy programs.

Just as the production increase was largely driven by rising oil prices, the trend could reverse if the global economy were to slow. Even so, much of the industry is thrilled at the prospects.

"To not be concerned with where our oil is going to come from is probably the biggest home run for the country in a hundred years," said Scott D. Sheffield, chief executive of Pioneer Natural Resources, which is operating in West Texas. "It sort of reminds me of the industrial revolution in coal, which allowed us to have some of the cheapest energy in the world and drove our economy in the late 1800s and 1900s."

THE FOUNDATION IS LAID

For as long as roughnecks have worked the Permian Basin — made famous during World War II as the fuel pump that powered the Allies — they have mostly focused on relatively shallow zones of easily accessible, oil-soaked sandstone and silt. But after 80 years of pumping, those regions were running dry.

So in 2003, Jim Henry, a West Texas oilman, tried a bold experiment. Borrowing an idea from a fellow engineer, his team at Henry Petroleum drilled deep into a hard limestone formation using a refinement of fracking. By blasting millions of gallons of water into the limestone, they created tiny fissures that allowed oil to break free, a technique that had previously been successful in extracting gas from shale.

The test produced 150 barrels of oil a day, three times more than normal. “We knew we had the biggest discovery in over 50 years in the Permian Basin,” Mr. Henry recalled.

There was just one problem: At $30 a barrel, the price of oil was about half of what was needed to make drilling that deep really profitable.

So the renaissance of the Permian — and the domestic oil industry — would have to wait.

But the drillers in Texas had important allies in Washington. President Bush grew up in Midland and spent 11 years as a West Texas oilman, albeit without much success, before entering politics. Vice President Dick Cheney had been chief executive of the oil field contractor Halliburton. The Bush administration worked from the start on finding ways to unlock the nation’s energy reserves and reverse decades of declining output, with Mr. Cheney leading a White House energy task force that met in secret with top oil executives.

“Ramping up production was a high priority,” said Gale Norton, a member of the task force and the secretary of the Interior at the time. “We hated being at the mercy of other countries, and we were determined to change that.”

The task force’s work helped produce the Energy Policy Act of 2005, which set rules that contributed to the current surge. It prohibited the Environmental Protection Agency from regulating fracking under the Safe Drinking Water Act, eliminating a potential impediment to wide use of the technique. The legislation also offered the industry billions of dollars in new tax breaks to help independent producers recoup some drilling costs even when a well came up dry.

Separately, the Interior Department was granted the power to issue drilling permits on millions of acres of federal lands without extensive environmental impact studies for individual projects, addressing industry complaints about the glacial pace of approvals. That new power has been used at least 8,400 times, mostly in Wyoming, Utah and New Mexico, representing a quarter of all permits issued on federal land in the last six federal fiscal years.

The Bush administration also opened large swaths of the Gulf of Mexico and the waters off Alaska to exploration, granting lease deals that required companies to pay only a tiny share of their profits to the government.

These measures primed the pump for the burst in drilling that began once oil prices started rising sharply in 2005 and 2006. With the world economy humming — and China, India and other developing nations posting astonishing growth — demand for oil began outpacing the easily accessible supplies.

By 2008, daily global oil consumption surged to 86 million barrels, up nearly 20 percent from the decade before. In July of that year, the price of oil reached its highest level since World War II, topping $145 a barrel (equivalent to more than $151 a barrel in today's dollars).

Oil reserves once too difficult and expensive to extract — including Mr. Henry's limestone fields — had become more attractive.

If money was the motivation, fracking became the favored means of extraction.

While fracking itself had been around for years, natural gas drillers in the 1980s and 1990s began combining high-pressure fracking with drilling wells horizontally, not just vertically. They found it unlocked gas from layers of shale previously seen as near worthless.

By 2001, fracking took off around Fort Worth and Dallas, eventually reaching under schools, airports and inner-city neighborhoods. Companies began buying drilling rights across vast shale fields in a variety of states. By 2008, the country was awash in natural gas.

Fracking for oil, which is made of larger molecules than natural gas, took longer to develop. But eventually, it opened new oil fields in North Dakota, South Texas, Kansas, Wyoming, Colorado and, most recently, Ohio.

Meanwhile, technological advances were making deeper oil drilling possible in the Gulf of Mexico. New imaging and seismic technology allowed engineers to predict the location and size of reservoirs once obscured by thick layers of salt. And drill bits made of superstrong alloys were developed to withstand the hot temperatures and high pressures deep under the seabed.

As the industry's confidence — and profits — grew, so did criticism. Amid concerns about global warming and gasoline prices that averaged a record $4.11 a gallon in July 2008 ($4.30 in today's dollars), President Obama campaigned on a pledge to shift toward renewable energy and away from fossil fuels.

His administration initially canceled some oil and gas leases on federal land awarded during the Bush administration and required more environmental review. But in a world where crucial oil suppliers like Venezuela and Libya were unstable and high energy prices could be a drag on a weak economy, he soon acted to promote more drilling. Despite a drilling hiatus after the 2010 explosion of the Deepwater Horizon in the Gulf of Mexico, which killed 11 rig workers and spilled millions of barrels of crude oil into the ocean, he has proposed expansion of oil production both on land and offshore. He is now moving toward approving drilling off the coast of Alaska.

"Our dependence on foreign oil is down because of policies put in place by our administration, but also our predecessor's administration," Mr. Obama said during a campaign appearance in March, a few weeks after opening 38 million more acres in the gulf for oil and gas exploration. "And whoever succeeds me is going to have to keep it up."

AN AMERICAN OIL BOOM

The last time the Permian Basin oil fields enjoyed a boom — nearly three decades ago — Rolls-Royce opened a showroom in the desert, Champagne was poured from cowboy boots, and the local airport could not accommodate all the Learjets taking off for Las Vegas on weekends.

But when crude prices fell in the mid-1980s, oil companies pulled out and the Rolls dealership was replaced by a tortilla factory. The only thriving business was done by bankruptcy lawyers and auctioneers helping to unload used Ferraris, empty homes and useless rigs.

"One day we were rolling in oil," recalled Jim Foreman, the general manager of the Midland BMW dealership, "and the next day geologists were flipping burgers at McDonald's."

The burger-flipping days are definitely over. Today, more than 475 rigs — roughly a quarter of all rigs operating in the United States — are smashing through tight rocks across the Permian in West Texas and southeastern New Mexico. Those areas are already producing nearly a million barrels a day, or 17 percent more than two years ago. By decade's end, that daily total could easily double, oil executives say, roughly equaling the total output of Nigeria.

"We're having a revolution," said G. Steven Farris, chief executive of Apache Corporation, one of the basin's most active producers. "And we're just scratching the surface."

It is a revolution that is returning investments to the United States. Over several decades, Pioneer Natural Resources had taken roughly $1 billion earned in Texas oil fields and drilled in Africa, South America and elsewhere. But in the last five years, the company sold $2 billion of overseas assets and reinvested in Texas shale fields.

"Political risk was increasing internationally," said Mr. Sheffield, Pioneer's chief executive, and domestically, he was encouraged to see "the shale technology progressing."

Pioneer's rising fortunes can be seen on a 10,000-acre field known as the Giddings Estate, a forsaken stretch inhabited by straggly coyotes, rabbits, rattlesnakes and cows that forage for grass between the sagebrush. When Pioneer bought it in 2005, the field's hundred mostly broken-down wells were producing a total of 50 barrels a day. "It was a diamond in the rough," said Robert Hillger, who manages it for Pioneer.

Mr. Hillger and his colleagues have brought an array of new tools to bear at Giddings. Computer programs simulate well designs, minimizing trial and error. Advanced fiber optics allow senior engineers and geologists at headquarters more than 300 miles away to monitor progress and remotely direct the drill bit. Subterranean microphones help identify fissures in the rock to plan subsequent drilling.

Today, the Giddings field is pumping 7,000 barrels a day, and Pioneer expects to hit 25,000 barrels a day by 2017.

The newfound wealth is spreading beyond the fields. In nearby towns, petroleum companies are buying so many pickup trucks that dealers are leasing parking lots the size of city blocks to stock their inventory. Housing is in such short supply that drillers are importing contractors from Houston and hotels are leased out before they are even built.

Two new office buildings are going up in Midland, a city of just over 110,000 people, the first in 30 years, while the total value of downtown real estate has jumped 50 percent since 2008. With virtually no unemployment, restaurants cannot find enough servers. Local truck drivers are making six-figure salaries.

"Anybody who comes in with a driver's license and a Social Security card, I'll give him a chance," said Rusty Allred, owner of Rusty's Oilfield Service Company.

If there is a loser in this boom, it is the environment. Water experts say aquifers in the desert area could run dry if fracking continues expanding, and oil executives concede they need to reduce water consumption. Yet environmental concerns, from polluted air to greenhouse gas emissions, have gained little traction in the Permian Basin or other outposts of the energy expansion.

On the front lines in opposition is Jay Lininger, a 36-year-old ecologist who drives through the Permian in an old Toyota Tacoma with a hard hat tilted on his head and a federal land map at the ready.

A former national park firefighter, he says he is now battling a wildfire of a different sort — the oil industry.

Nationally, environmentalists have challenged drilling with mixed results. Efforts to stop or slow fracking have succeeded in New York State and some localities in other states, but it is spreading across the country.

In the Permian, Mr. Lininger said, few people openly object to the foul-smelling air of the oil fields. Ranchers are more than happy to sell what water they have to the oil companies for fracking.

Mr. Lininger and his group are trying to slow the expansion of drilling by appealing to the United States Fish and Wildlife Service to protect several animal species, including the five-inch dunes sagebrush lizard.

"It's a pathetic little lizard in an ugly desert, but life needs to be protected," he said. "Every day we burn fossil fuel makes it harder for our planet to recover from our energy addiction."

Mr. Lininger said the oil and ranching industries had already destroyed or fragmented 40 percent of the lizard's habitat, and 60 percent of what is left is under lease for oil and gas development.

The wildlife agency proposed listing the lizard as endangered in 2010 and was expected to decide last December, but Congressional representatives from the oil patch won a delay. Oil companies are working on a voluntary program to locate new drilling so it will not disturb the lizard habitat.

But for Mr. Lininger's group, the Center for Biological Diversity, that is far from sufficient.

Brendan Cummings, senior counsel of the center, said protecting the lizard was part of a broader effort to keep drilling from harming animals, including polar bears, walruses and bowhead whales in the Alaskan Arctic and dwarf sea horses and sea turtles in the Gulf of Mexico.

"When you are dealing with fossil fuels, things will always go wrong," Mr. Cummings said. "There will always be spills, there will always be pollution. Those impacts compound the fragmentation that occurs and render these habitats into sacrifice areas."

A TURN TOWARD EFFICIENCY

If the Permian Basin exemplifies the rise in production, car-obsessed San Diego is a prime example of the other big factor in the decline in the nation's reliance on foreign oil.

Just since 2007, consumption of all liquid fuels in the United States, including diesel, jet fuel and heating oil, has dropped by about 9 percent, according to the Energy Department. Gasoline use fell 6 to 12 percent, estimated Tom Kloza, chief oil analyst at the Oil Price Information Service.

Although Southern California's love affair with muscle cars and the open road persists, driving habits have changed in subtle but important ways.

Take Tory Girten, who works as an emergency medical technician and part-time lifeguard in the San Diego area. He switched from driving a Ford minivan to a decidedly smaller and more fuel-efficient Dodge Caliber. Fed up with high gasoline prices, he also moved twice recently to be closer to the city center, cutting his daily commute considerably — a hint of the shift taking place in certain metropolitan areas as city centers become more popular while growth in far-out suburbs slows.

"I would rather pay a little more monthly for rent than for just filling up my tank with gas," he said, after pulling into a local gas station to fill up.

Mr. Girten is one of millions of Americans who have downsized. S.U.V.'s accounted for 18 percent of new-car sales in 2002, but only 7 percent in 2010.

The surge in gasoline prices nationwide — they are already at a record level for this time of year — has contributed to the shift toward more fuel-efficient cars. But a bigger factor is rising federal fuel economy standards. After a long freeze, the miles-per-gallon mandate has been increased several times in recent years, with the Obama administration now pushing automakers to hit 54.5 m.p.g. by 2025.

As Americans replace their older cars — they have bought an average of 1.25 million new cars and light trucks a month this year — new technologies mean they usually end up with a more efficient vehicle, even if they buy a model of similar size and power.

California has long pushed further and faster toward efficiency than the rest of the country. It has combated often severe air pollution by mandating cleaner-burning cars, including all-electric vehicles, and prodded Washington to increase the fuel efficiency standards.

Thousands of school buses, trash trucks, tractor-trailers and street sweepers and public transit buses in the state run on natural gas, which is cheaper than gasoline and burns more cleanly. That switch cuts the consumption of foreign oil, as does the corn-based ethanol that is now mixed into gasoline as a result of federal mandates.

Longer-term social and economic factors are also reducing miles driven — like the rise in Internet shopping and telecommuting and the tendency of baby boomers to drive less as they age. The recession has also contributed, as job losses have meant fewer daily commutes and falling home prices have allowed some people to afford to move closer to work.

The trend of lower consumption, when combined with higher energy production, has profound implications, said Bill White, former deputy energy secretary in the Clinton administration and former mayor of Houston.

"Energy independence has always been a race between depletion and technologies to produce more and use energy more efficiently," he said. "Depletion was winning for decades, and now technology is starting to overtake its lead."

CLIFFORD KRAUSS reported from Midland, Tex., and Houston and **ERIC LIPTON** reported from Washington and San Diego. **JOHN M. BRODER** contributed reporting from Washington.

A Brighter Future for Electric Cars and the Planet

EDITORIAL | BY THE NEW YORK TIMES | JULY 18, 2017

THERE IS SIMPLY no credible way to address climate change without changing the way we get from here to there, meaning cars, trucks, planes and any other gas-guzzling forms of transportation. That is why it is so heartening to see electric cars, considered curios for the rich or eccentric or both not that long ago, now entering the mainstream.

A slew of recent announcements by researchers, auto companies and world leaders offer real promise. First up, a forecast by Bloomberg New Energy Finance said that electric cars would become cheaper than conventional cars without government subsidies between 2025 and 2030. At the same time, auto companies like Tesla, General Motors and Volvo are planning a slate of new models that they say will be not only more affordable but also more practical than earlier versions. And officials in such countries as France, India and Norway have set aggressive targets for putting these vehicles to use and phasing out emission-spewing gasoline and diesel cars.

Skeptics may see these announcements as wishful thinking. After all, just 1.1 percent of all cars sold globally in 2016 were electrics or plug-in hybrids. And many popular models still cost much more than comparable fossil-fuel cars.

The skeptics, however, have consistently been overly pessimistic about this technology. Electric cars face challenges, yet they have caught on much faster than was thought likely just a few years ago. There were two million of them on the world's roads last year, up 60 percent from 2015, according to the International Energy Agency. The cost of batteries, the single most expensive component of the cars, fell by more than half between 2012 and 2016, according to the Department of Energy. Tesla has indicated that it can produce batteries for about $125 per kilowatt-hour. Researchers say the cost of electric cars will be at parity with conventional vehicles when battery prices reach $100 per kilowatt-hour, which experts say is just a few years away. Electric cars are more efficient, of course, but they also require less maintenance, which should make them cheaper to own over time.

The potential environmental benefits of electric vehicles are huge. The transportation sector accounts for 14 percent of global greenhouse gas emissions and 27 percent of emissions in the United States. Moreover, countries have found it much more difficult to reduce planet-warming gases from transportation than from power plants. In America, for example, transportation emissions again regularly exceed those from the electricity sector for the first time since the late 1970s. The switch to electric cars is good for the climate because petroleum vehicles produce more greenhouse gas emissions per unit of energy than power plants fueled by natural gas, according to the Energy Information Administration. Proponents say the growth of electric cars, when combined with the surge in renewable energy sources, like solar and wind, could lead to big reductions in emissions over time. These forces should also help reduce local air pollution in countries like China and India, which is why their leaders are getting behind these technologies in a big way. Government incentives have turned China into the biggest market for electric vehicles. And an Indian government minister says his country wants all cars sold there by 2030 to be electric. France says it wants to end sales of new diesel and gasoline cars by 2040, while Norway's goal is 2025.

Government support could prove as crucial to the future of the technology as technical advances. If countries, states and localities encourage the spread of public charging stations, through tax breaks, other incentives or public spending, more people will take the plunge and convert. If the United States and other governments continue to spend money on research to help drive down battery costs, their economies and consumers will benefit.

Some parts of the fossil fuel industry will no doubt try to sabotage the electric car revolution. In the United States, the industry is lobbying states to eliminate subsidies for the vehicles. And many analysts expect the industry to seek similar changes at the federal level from President Trump and Republican leaders in Congress, who have already made clear that they do not see climate change as a major threat. They should know, though, that the most they can do is slow down the process. The electric car has already left the garage.

What Needs to Happen Before Electric Cars Take Over the World

BY JACK EWING | DEC. 18, 2017

Electric vehicles have only a tiny market share, but the auto industry is betting billions that they will soon be as cheap as conventional cars.

ON THE SLOPE of a thickly forested Czech mountain, three men in hard hats and mud-spattered fluorescent vests dig for the metal that could power a new industrial revolution.

They watch carefully as a mobile rig, mounted on tank treads, hammers and spins a drill bit hundreds of yards into the bedrock. Water gushes from the bore as the bit punctures an underground spring.

The men are prospecting for new sources of lithium, a raw material

GORDON WELTERS FOR THE NEW YORK TIMES

Workers at a drilling site in the Czech Republic.

now found primarily in China and Chile that could become as important to the auto industry as oil is now.

Faster than anyone expected, electric cars are becoming as economical and practical as cars with conventional engines. Prices for lithium-ion batteries are plummeting, while technical advances are increasing driving ranges and cutting recharging times.

"Once the trend gets going, it can happen very fast," said Guido Jouret, chief digital officer at ABB, an electronics company based in Zurich whose businesses include constructing charging stations.

But this electric-car future is still missing some pieces. Some crucial raw materials are scarce. There are not enough places to recharge. Battery-powered cars still cost thousands of dollars more than many gasoline vehicles.

Car companies are racing to overcome these obstacles. They, and the millions of people they employ, risk becoming irrelevant.

"Many people are nervous about how fast this is coming and how much they have to invest," said Norbert Dressler, a senior partner at Roland Berger in Stuttgart, Germany, who advises the auto industry.

Here's a look at what needs to happen before electric cars take over the world.

The cost of building motors and components will have to continue to decrease.

Price of an electric powertrain:
$16,000
Price of a conventional car powertrain:
$6,000

Electric cars will go mainstream when the cost of the powertrain — the motor and other guts that make the vehicle move — is the same as owning cars that burn gasoline or diesel. How soon that day arrives is almost solely a function of the price of batteries.

Battery prices, measured by the power they produce, have already fallen by more than half since 2011, according to analysts at Bank of America Merrill Lynch. The unexpectedly rapid drop in prices has sped up the timetable.

Merrill Lynch analysts now expect electric vehicles in the United States will be cheaper than their traditional counterparts by 2024. Just a year ago, they estimated it would take until 2030.

One reason battery costs are falling is that manufacturers are ramping up production. The greater the supply, the lower the price.

Car companies like Daimler are getting into the battery business. Daimler has invested $590 million in a new battery plant in Kamenz, a sleepy city in a rural part of eastern Germany.

"This is an important investment in the future," Chancellor Angela Merkel told Daimler executives and other dignitaries at a groundbreaking in May. Within a few months, workers had erected prefabricated concrete walls for the enormous new building and assembled the roof girders.

"We could buy batteries," said Jupp Kaufer, head of quality at Accumotive, Daimler's battery unit.

But Daimler would rather earn the profits than pay them to a supplier like Samsung or Panasonic. "The battery is a crucial part of the vehicle," Mr. Kaufer said as he walked through the assembly line of another factory in Kamenz that is already running at capacity.

There must be a steady, affordable supply of the resources required to make batteries.

Price of cobalt:

Up 115 percent this year

Price of lithium:

Up 45 percent

Price of graphite:

Up 30 percent

Carmakers are racing to secure the essential ingredients in batteries like cobalt, lithium and graphite. They need to avoid shortages that would drive prices too high, making electric vehicles unaffordable.

But manufacturers are also dealing with a geopolitical dimension. Three-quarters of the world's reserves of lithium, a crucial ingredient in the most common kind of electric car battery, are in China and Chile, according to the United States Geological Survey. As demand surges, China could deploy its natural resources as a diplomatic cudgel the same way that Saudi Arabia uses oil.

The risk that a few countries could control most of the ingredients for electric car batteries is what spurred the drilling crew to the mountainside in Cinovec in the Czech Republic. As early as the 1300s, miners dug tin — "cin" in Czech — from the mountains around the town. Later, the area was an important source of tungsten, but the last shaft closed in 1993. Demand for lithium has made mining in the area attractive again.

European Metals Holdings Ltd., an Australian company, is drilling into the bedrock and hauling out core samples to map deposits.

The company plans to complete a feasibility study next year and begin mining and processing the ore in Cinovec soon after.

"We are already in touch with some battery makers," Richard Pavlik, manager of a European Metals subsidiary overseeing the work in Cinovec, said as he watched the drilling crew.

As for cobalt, it comes primarily from the Democratic Republic of Congo, one of the world's most war-torn and unstable countries. Illegal mining operations there have been accused of using child labor.

Mining companies are hunting for sources in less problematic locations. First Cobalt, based in Toronto, has announced plans to reopen a former silver and cobalt mine in the aptly named town of Cobalt, Ontario. "We think we are at a point of no return with electric vehicles," said Trent Mell, the company's chief executive.

More charging stations will need to be built, and they'll need to charge faster.

Average range of a gasoline-powered car:
475 miles

Average range of an electric vehicle:
190 miles

Even when people can buy an electric car for the same price or less than a gasoline model, they face another problem: where to plug it in. And they won't want to wait all day for the car to recharge.

Electric cars will become commonplace once there is a dense network of high-voltage charging stations where drivers can refill their batteries in the time it takes to use the restroom and drink a cup of coffee.

At the moment, a cross-country drive in an electric car is an adventure.

JASON HENRY FOR THE NEW YORK TIMES

A Tesla owner charging his car at a station in Mountain View, Calif., earlier this year.

Edwin Stafford, a professor of marketing at Utah State University in Logan, Utah, carefully plotted his charging stops before setting out recently in his Tesla S for Berkeley, Calif., with his family.

Tesla S owners have free access to Tesla charging stations and can use the waiting time to have a meal or shop. In half an hour, a high voltage Tesla "supercharger" can supply enough juice to travel 170 miles, according to Tesla. But the amenities at charging stations varied, Mr. Stafford said.

At one in Nevada, the only nearby business was a casino, he said. At another, the charging apparatus was blocked by an illegally parked truck. Close to the Bay Area, there were sometimes lines of other Tesla owners waiting to charge, he added.

But an array of start-ups and established companies like ABB are busy installing charging stations around the world, and they are on their way to becoming commonplace. There are already about 16,000 public charging stations in the United States, up from a few hundred in 2010. That compares with about 112,000 gas stations.

Surprisingly, Volkswagen's emissions scandal has accelerated the rollout. As part of its settlement with diesel owners in the United States who bought cars with illegal software, Volkswagen agreed to spend $2 billion to promote electric cars and build infrastructure. Electrify America, a company established to invest the settlement money, plans to install more than 2,000 fast chargers nationwide by mid-2019 in a first phase, with thousands more to follow.

Drivers will have to shed their attachment to the sound, smell and feel of gas-powered engines.

Time from 0 to 60 m.p.h, Audi A8:
4 seconds

Time from 0 to 60 m.p.h, Tesla S:
2.3 seconds

One of the biggest barriers for electric vehicles is psychological. People are used to internal combustion engines and the sensations that go with them — the odor of the fuel, the shifting of the transmission, the sound of the engine as the car accelerates.

Electric cars have a different personality that people need to get their heads around before they will buy one.

They may be pleasantly surprised. The physics of electric motors give them exceptional acceleration. A $135,000 Tesla S clocked by Motor Trend magazine went from zero to 60 miles per hour faster than Ferraris, Lamborghinis or Porsches costing hundreds of thousands of dollars more.

Electric cars are quiet, nearly vibration free and they don't smell like gasoline or exhaust. They don't need oil changes. They cost less to operate — around 4 cents per mile compared with 10 cents per mile for a gasoline-powered car, depending on local costs for electricity and fuel, which often fluctuate. Electric cars hug the road because heavy battery packs, typically arrayed underneath the passenger compartment, provide low centers of gravity and high stability.

"There is no question that an electric car gives you significantly better performance," Mr. Stafford said. "I don't think the mainstream driver is going to understand that unless they experience it."

The car industry will have to leave some of its old methods of production by the side of the road.

Carmakers' investment in electric vehicles:

$100 billion by 2020

Carmakers' annual profit:

$400 billion

The industry is racing to invest in the future, as electric cars portend sweeping economic and societal changes. The transition will be painful for traditional carmakers and suppliers, potentially even catastrophic.

Electric cars have about 25 percent fewer parts than conventional autos. Companies that make engine parts like pistons, fuel injection systems or spark plugs will have to find new products to sell, or die. Some workers' skills will no longer be needed.

Governments will lose fuel tax revenues. Filling stations and auto repair shops will go out of business. To compete with Tesla, which allows customers to buy cars online, car companies will have to radically streamline their dealership networks.

"The cake will be smaller," said Volkmar Denner, the chief executive of Bosch, the auto parts maker.

Established carmakers will face new competitors taking advantage of the technology shift to break into the market. Chinese companies are investing heavily in electric cars. Dyson, a British company hitherto known for its innovative vacuum cleaners, has announced plans to develop an electric car.

Big car companies recognize the threat and argue that they can deploy their enormous manufacturing networks to roll out electric vehicles faster than Tesla, which has struggled to meet demand.

"We won't have a problem building one million cars," said Herbert Diess, chief executive of the division that makes Volkswagen brand cars.

But the automakers' existing expertise — building internal combustion engines — will no longer give them a competitive edge.

"They are losing a lot of their intellectual capital," said Geoffrey Heal, a professor at Columbia Business School. "And they have to find a way to replace it."

Glossary

boom A moment of prosperity or rapid growth.

climate change Generally refers to the disruption and shifting of climate patterns as a result of human industrial practices in the past centuries.

commodity A primary resource or material that can be bought and sold in a market.

efficiency Work to energy ratio; higher efficiency means a system can do more work with less energy spent.

emission The output of a system; usually refers to waste, pollution or a byproduct.

fossil fuel Carbon-based energy sources formed from organic matter millions of years old; includes petroleum, oil, natural gas, and coal.

fracking A nickname for hydraulic fracturing, a process of pumping high-pressure bursts of water and chemicals into shale rock in order to force the shale oil out into a well.

geopolitics The set of power relationships among nations around the world.

geothermal Heat from inside the earth. This heat can sometimes be used to drive turbines that create electricity.

hydroelectric Related to generating power by using flowing water to drive a turbine.

infrastructure The facilities and structures required by a project or a civilization, e.g. roads, bridges, electrical grids, oil pipelines.

kilowatt-hour Electrical energy measurement equivalent to 1,000 watts for 1 hour.

nuclear fission The process of breaking apart the nucleus of an atom, resulting in a large release of energy. In an uncontrolled chain reaction, the result is a nuclear explosion. The controlled version happens in a nuclear power plant.

nuclear fusion The process of fusing subatomic particles into a new nucleus, also resulting in a large release of energy. Hydrogen bombs are uncontrolled fusion reactions, as is the burning fire of the sun. Controlled nuclear fusion is very difficult to achieve and a long-time goal of modern science.

offshore drilling The process of drilling oil wells under the seabed.

parabolic Shaped like a parabola, or a part of a parabola.

renaissance A revival or flourishing of an activity or style.

reservoir A large ready supply; usually a place where fluids collect or a place where fluids are stored.

seismic Having to do with earthquakes or vibrations in the ground.

shale oil Crude oil that is trapped between layers of shale rock, deep underground.

subsidy A financial grant by the government to an industry in order to keep prices artificially low.

synthetic Something made by combining chemicals, usually to imitate something natural.

Media Literacy Terms

"Media literacy" refers to the ability to access, understand, critically assess and create media. The following terms are important components of media literacy, and they will help you critically engage with the articles in this title.

angle The aspect of a news story that a journalist focuses on and develops.

attribution The method by which a source is identified or by which facts and information are assigned to the person who provided them.

balance Principle of journalism that both perspectives of an argument should be presented in a fair way.

byline Name of the writer, usually placed between the headline and the story.

chronological order Method of writing a story presenting the details of the story in the order in which they occurred.

commentary A type of story that is an expression of opinion on recent events by a journalist generally known as a commentator.

credibility The quality of being trustworthy and believable, said of a journalistic source.

editorial Article of opinion or interpretation.

fake news A fictional or made-up story presented in the style of a legitimate news story, intended to deceive readers; also commonly used to criticize legitimate news because of its perspective or unfavorable coverage of a subject.

feature story Article designed to entertain as well as to inform.

human interest story A type of story that focuses on individuals and how events or issues affect their lives, generally offering a sense of relatability to the reader.

impartiality Principle of journalism that a story should not reflect a journalist's bias and should contain balance.

intention The motive or reason behind something, such as the publication of a news story.

motive The reason behind something, such as the publication of a news story or a source's perspective on an issue.

news story An article or style of expository writing that reports news, generally in a straightforward fashion and without editorial comment.

op-ed An opinion piece that reflects a prominent individual's opinion on a topic of interest.

paraphrase The summary of an individual's words, with attribution, rather than a direct quotation of their exact words.

quotation The use of an individual's exact words indicated by the use of quotation marks and proper attribution.

reliability The quality of being dependable and accurate, said of a journalistic source.

rhetorical device Technique in writing intending to persuade the reader or communicate a message from a certain perspective.

source The origin of the information reported in journalism.

style A distinctive use of language in writing or speech; also a news or publishing organization's rules for consistent use of language with regard to spelling, punctuation, typography and capitalization, usually regimented by a house style guide.

tone A manner of expression in writing or speech.

Media Literacy Questions

1. What is the intention of the article "Meeting the Energy Dilemma" (on page 25)? How effectively does it achieve its intended purpose?

2. Analyze the authors' reporting in "Oil Exacts a Price From the Earth" (on page 49) and "Lessons From the Exxon Valdez Oil Spill" (on page 68). Do you think one journalist is more balanced in his reporting than the other? If so, why do you think so?

3. What is the intention of the article "A War for Oil?" (on page 55)? How effectively does it achieve its intended purpose?

4. "Where Wind Farms Meet Coal Country, There's Enduring Faith in Trump" (on page 135) features several photographs. What do these photographs add to the article?

5. Does "New Technologies Redraw the World's Energy Picture" (on page 176) use multiple sources? What are the strengths of using multiple sources in a journalistic piece? What are the weaknesses of relying heavily on only one or a few sources?

6. The article "Nuclear Fallout" (on page 167) is an example of an op-ed. Identify how Kristen Iversen's attitude and tone help convey her opinion on the topic.

7. What type of story is "What Needs to Happen Before Electric Cars Take Over the World" (on page 203)? Can you identify another article in this collection that is the same type of story? What elements helped you come to your conclusion?

8. Compare the headlines of "Role of Nuclear Power Is Disputed Despite Looming Energy Shortage" (on page 164) and "Nuclear Power's Death Somewhat Exaggerated" (on page 170). Which is a more compelling headline, and why? How could the less compelling headline be changed to better draw the reader's interest?

9. Identify the various sources cited in the article "Even in Coal Country, the Fight for an Industry" (on page 115). How does Eric Lipton attribute information to each of these sources in the article? How effective are Lipton's attributions in helping the reader identify his sources?

10. The article "Coal Museum Sees the Future; Trump Doesn't" (on page 131) is an example of an op-ed. Identify how Thomas L. Friedman's attitude and tone help convey his opinion on the topic.

11. Analyze the authors' reporting in "Studies Say Natural Gas Has Its Own Environmental Problems" (on page 92) and "Natural Gas Signals a 'Manufacturing Renaissance' " (on page 109). Do you think one journalist is more impartial in his reporting than the other? If so, why do you think so?

Citations

All citations in this list are formatted according to the Modern Language Association's (MLA) style guide.

BOOK CITATION

THE NEW YORK TIMES EDITORIAL STAFF. *Energy Technology: The Tools of the Industry*. New York: New York Times Educational Publishing, 2020.

ONLINE ARTICLE CITATIONS

DANIELS, FARRINGTON. "A Limitless Resource: Solar Energy." *The New York Times*, 18 Mar. 1956, https://www.nytimes.com/1956/03/18/archives/a-limitless-resource-solar-energy-in-a-world-that-needs-more-and.html.

DANIELS, LEE A. "As Gulf War Intensifies, Oil Price Worries Grow." *The New York Times*, 26 Jan. 1987, https://www.nytimes.com/1987/01/26/business/as-gulf-war-intensifies-oil-price-worries-grow.html.

ELLIOTT, REBECCA. "In Hurricane Harvey's Wake, We Need a Green 'New Deal.' " *The New York Times*, 20 Jan. 2018, https://www.nytimes.com/2017/08/31/opinion/in-hurricane-harveys-wake-we-need-a-green-new-deal.html.

EWING, JACK. "What Needs to Happen Before Electric Cars Take Over the World." *The New York Times*, 22 Jan. 2018, https://www.nytimes.com/2017/12/18/business/electric-car-adoption.html.

FOUNTAIN, HENRY. "Lessons From the Exxon Valdez Oil Spill." *The New York Times*, 19 Oct. 2018, https://www.nytimes.com/2013/12/09/booming/lessons-from-the-exxon-valdez-oil-spill.html.

FOUNTAIN, HENRY. "U.S. Acts to Spur Development of High-Tech Reactors." *The New York Times*, 21 Dec. 2017, https://www.nytimes.com/2016/01/20/science/advanced-nuclear-reactors-department-of-energy.html.

FRIEDMAN, THOMAS L. "Coal Museum Sees the Future; Trump Doesn't." *The New York Times*, 20 Jan. 2018, https://www.nytimes.com/2017/04/19/opinion/coal-museum-sees-the-future-trump-doesnt.html.

FRIEDMAN, THOMAS L. "The Green New Deal Rises Again." *The New York Times*, 11 Jan. 2019, https://www.nytimes.com/2019/01/08/opinion/green-new-deal.html.

FRIEDMAN, THOMAS L. "A War for Oil?" *The New York Times*, 5 Jan. 2003, https://www.nytimes.com/2003/01/05/opinion/a-war-for-oil.html.

GALBRAITH, KATE. "Dash for Gas Raises Environmental Worries." *The New York Times*, 12 July 2010, https://www.nytimes.com/2010/07/12/business/energy-environment/12iht-green.html.

GARDINER, BETH. "In Europe, the Promise and Fears of a New Fuel." *The New York Times*, 22 Feb. 2011, https://www.nytimes.com/2011/02/21/business/energy-environment/21iht-renoshale21.html.

HICKS, NANCY. "Scientists Warn Atom Power Foes." *The New York Times*, 16 Aug. 1970, https://www.nytimes.com/1970/08/16/archives/scientists-warn-atom-power-foes-say-public-must-back-gains-or-give.html.

IVERSEN, KRISTEN. "Nuclear Fallout." *The New York Times*, 10 Mar. 2012, https://www.nytimes.com/2012/03/11/opinion/sunday/fallout-at-a-former-nuclear-weapon-plant.html.

JENKINS, JESSE, AND SAMUEL THERNSTROM. "We Need More Than Solar and Wind to Power the Green New Deal." *The New York Times*, 18 Jan. 2019, https://www.nytimes.com/2019/01/17/opinion/green-new-deal-climate-change.html.

KANTER, JAMES. "A White-Hot Future for Oil and Gas." *The New York Times*, 10 Oct. 2011, https://www.nytimes.com/2011/10/11/business/energy-environment/a-white-hot-future-for-oil-and-gas.html.

KRAUSS, CLIFFORD. "Coal's Decline Seems Impervious to Trump's Promises." *The New York Times*, 17 Oct. 2018, https://www.nytimes.com/2018/01/24/business/energy-environment/coal-miners.html.

KRAUSS, CLIFFORD. "In North Dakota, Flames of Wasted Natural Gas Light the Prairie." *The New York Times*, 26 Sept. 2011, https://www.nytimes.com/2011/09/27/business/energy-environment/in-north-dakota-wasted-natural-gas-flickers-against-the-sky.html.

KRAUSS, CLIFFORD. "New Technologies Redraw the World's Energy Picture." *The New York Times*, 25 Oct. 2011, https://www.nytimes.com/2011/10/26/business/energy-environment/new-technologies-redraw-the-worlds-energy-picture.html.

KRAUSS, CLIFFORD. "Shale Boom in Texas Could Increase U.S. Oil Output." *The New York Times*, 27 May 2011, https://www.nytimes.com/2011/05/28/business/energy-environment/28shale.html.

KRAUSS, CLIFFORD. "Where Wind Farms Meet Coal Country, There's

Enduring Faith in Trump." *The New York Times*, 14 Dec. 2017, https://www.nytimes.com/interactive/2017/12/14/business/economy/trump-coal-alternative-energy.html.

KRAUSS, CLIFFORD, AND MICHAEL CORKERY. "A Bleak Outlook for Trump's Promises to Coal Miners." *The New York Times*, 20 Jan. 2018, https://www.nytimes.com/2016/11/20/business/energy-environment/a-bleak-outlook-for-trumps-promises-to-coal-miners.html.

KRAUSS, CLIFFORD, AND ERIC LIPTON. "U.S. Inches Toward Goal of Energy Independence." *The New York Times*, 22 Mar. 2012, https://www.nytimes.com/2012/03/23/business/energy-environment/inching-toward-energy-independence-in-america.html.

LAURENCE, WILLIAM L. "New Solar Engine Gives Cheap Power." *The New York Times*, 30 Dec. 1935, https://www.nytimes.com/1935/12/30/archives/new-solar-engine-gives-cheap-power-smithsonian-secretary-shows.html.

LIPTON, ERIC. "Even in Coal Country, the Fight for an Industry." *The New York Times*, 29 May 2012, https://www.nytimes.com/2012/05/30/business/energy-environment/even-in-kentucky-coal-industry-is-under-siege.html.

MCLAUGHLIN, KATHLEEN. "U.S. Harnessing Volcanic Steam." *The New York Times*, 21 Oct. 1962, https://www.nytimes.com/1962/10/21/archives/us-harnessing-volcanic-steam-other-nations-also-active-in.html.

MOTAVALLI, JIM. "Natural Gas Signals a 'Manufacturing Renaissance.' " *The New York Times*, 10 Apr. 2012, https://www.nytimes.com/2012/04/11/business/energy-environment/wider-availability-expands-uses-for-natural-gas.html.

THE NEW YORK TIMES. "A Brighter Future for Electric Cars and the Planet." *The New York Times*, 20 Jan. 2018, https://www.nytimes.com/2017/07/18/opinion/a-brighter-future-for-electric-cars-and-the-planet.html.

THE NEW YORK TIMES. "Iraq Deploys Troops Near Kuwait Border Amid Dispute on Oil." *The New York Times*, 24 July 1990, https://www.nytimes.com/1990/07/24/world/iraq-deploys-troops-near-kuwait-border-amid-dispute-on-oil.html.

THE NEW YORK TIMES. "Meeting the Energy Dilemma." *The New York Times*, 20 July 1971, https://www.nytimes.com/1971/07/20/archives/meeting-the-energy-dilemma.html.

THE NEW YORK TIMES. "Role of Nuclear Power Is Disputed Despite Looming Energy Shortage." *The New York Times*, 2 Jan. 1990, https://www.nytimes.com/1990/01/02/us/role-of-nuclear-power-is-disputed-despite-looming-energy-shortage.html.

PLUMER, BRAD. "Trump's New Pollution Rules Still Won't Save the Coal

Industry." *The New York Times*, 23 Aug. 2018, https://www.nytimes.com/2018/08/22/climate/trump-coal-industry.html.

REED, STANLEY. "Oil Firms Learn to Move an Ancient Product With New-Age Tech." *The New York Times*, 20 Oct. 2017, https://www.nytimes.com/2017/10/14/business/energy-environment/oil-firms-learn-to-move-an-ancient-product-with-new-age-tech.html.

ROBERTSON, CAMPBELL, AND CLIFFORD KRAUSS. "BP May Be Fined Up to $18 Billion for Spill in Gulf." *The New York Times*, 19 Jan. 2018, https://www.nytimes.com/2014/09/05/business/bp-negligent-in-2010-oil-spill-us-judge-rules.html.

SCOTT, MARK. "Out of Africa (and Elsewhere): More Fossil Fuels." *The New York Times*, 10 Apr. 2012, https://www.nytimes.com/2012/04/11/business/energy-environment/quest-for-new-fossil-fuels-goes-to-africa-and-beyond.html.

SILLIN, LELAN F., JR. "A 30-Year Plan for Pollution-Free Energy Sources." *The New York Times*, 13 Dec. 1971, https://www.nytimes.com/1971/12/13/archives/a-30year-plan-for-pollutionfree-energy-sources.html.

SMITH, GENE. "Nuclear Power Arrives — Again." *The New York Times*, 29 Nov. 1970, https://www.nytimes.com/1970/11/29/archives/nuclear-power-arrives-again-utilities-1970-orders-of-aplants-soar.html.

SMITH, WILLIAM D. "Economic Analysis." *The New York Times*, 6 June 1972, https://www.nytimes.com/1972/06/06/archives/power-in-oil-world-vastly-different-since-1967-war-economic.html.

STEVENS, WILLIAM K. "Oil Exacts A Price From The Earth." *The New York Times*, 2 Apr. 1989, https://www.nytimes.com/1989/04/02/weekinreview/ideas-trends-oil-exacts-a-price-from-the-earth.html.

WALD, MATTHEW L. "Nuclear Power's Death Somewhat Exaggerated." *The New York Times*, 10 Apr. 2012, https://www.nytimes.com/2012/04/11/business/energy-environment/nuclear-powers-death-somewhat-exaggerated.html.

WALD, MATTHEW L. "Study Says Natural Gas Use Likely to Double." *The New York Times*, 25 June 2010, https://www.nytimes.com/2010/06/25/business/energy-environment/25natgas.html.

ZELLER, TOM, JR. "E.P.A. to Study Chemicals Used to Tap Natural Gas." *The New York Times*, 9 Sept. 2010, https://www.nytimes.com/2010/09/10/business/energy-environment/10hydraulic.html.

ZELLER, TOM, JR. "Studies Say Natural Gas Has Its Own Problems." *The New York Times*, 11 Apr. 2011, https://www.nytimes.com/2011/04/12/business/energy-environment/12gas.html.

Index

This book is current up until the time of printing. For the most up-to-date reporting, visit www.nytimes.com.